CW01506974

I'M NO EXPERT, BUT . . .

UNPUBLISHED LETTERS
TO

The Telegraph

EDITED BY KATE MOORE

Aurum

Quarto

First published in 2025 by Aurum Press,
an imprint of The Quarto Group.
One Triptych Place, London, SE1 9SH,
United Kingdom
T (0)20 7700 9000
www.Quarto.com

EEA Representation, WTS Tax d.o.o.,
Žanova ulica 3, 4000 Kranj, Slovenia
www.wts-tax.si

A catalogue record for this book is available from the British Library.

ISBN: 978-1-8360-0827-9
Ebook: 978-1-8360-0828-6

10 9 8 7 6 5 4 3 2 1

Typeset in Mrs Eaves by SX Composing DTP, Rayleigh, Essex

Printed and bound by CPI Group (UK) Ltd, Croydon, CR0 4YY 092025

CONTENTS

INTRODUCTION

Well, we can't say we weren't warned. In his first major speech as Prime Minister, weeks after winning a landslide victory at the general election, Sir Keir Starmer told a nervous nation that "things will get worse before they get better". More than a year on, the truth of that has been borne out, both in the headlines and in the correspondence that arrived on *The Daily Telegraph*'s Letters Desk. Disgusted of Tunbridge Wells, along with lesser-known cousins such as Angry of Upminster and Disgruntled of Henley-on-Thames, have had a particularly active year.

For Labour, the "worse" part of Sir Keir's prophecy began almost immediately. Rachel Reeves promptly dropped a boulder on the economy, then spent the ensuing months trying to restore confidence in her position as Chancellor. Meanwhile, with rebellion brewing on the back benches, the PM performed so many U-turns that motion sickness set in. The winter fuel payment, the grooming gangs inquiry, benefits reform, international aid spending, even the precise definition of a woman – there seemed to be no position robust enough to withstand a political squall. The drama was not confined to the governing party. While the Conservatives fretted over whether to oust their 137th leader in three years, Reform UK seized the advantage at the local elections. Was it perhaps the beginning of a Reform-nation, wondered one reader? Or the moment for a coalition ReformaTory party? Only time would tell.

There was plenty of upheaval elsewhere. Across the pond, President Trump set about demolishing liberal nostrums with a slew of executive orders. His defenders argued that he was, at least, carrying out promises he had made on the electoral trail: something rarely seen among British politicians. Harder to stomach was the sight of Mr Trump laying into Volodymyr Zelensky at the White House. Perhaps, one reader suggested, we had a new definition of "Trump derangement syndrome". At least the prospect of a state visit allowed outraged letter-writers to start plotting their own (scrupulously polite, of course) forms of retaliation.

With so much uncertainty in the air, it is good to know that, in some circles at least, a can-do spirit prevails. Even if those in charge were unable to come up with any viable solutions to the nation's problems, we could always rely on the *Telegraph*'s readers to step into the breach. One suggested that we might be better off replacing the Prime Minister with AI, as we had done with the line judges at Wimbledon. Others devised ingenious ways of securing the country's defences on the cheap (a quick trip to Argos should sort it). Negotiations with the EU going badly? Send in the car-traders. Net zero proving unpopular? Institute a ban on petrol-powered leaf blowers, and all will be well. Forthright, ingenious and always quick off the mark, the readers could certainly hold their own on the political stage.

For most of us not trapped in the Westminster bubble, life goes on away from politics. So it has for our correspondents. This year they have weathered a summer heatwave, roared on the Lionesses, rocked out at Glastonbury and put a brave face on the UK's defeat at Eurovision. They have passed judgment on an array of public figures, sparing neither sporting royalty (Sir David Beckham, Gary Lineker) nor actual royalty (the Duke of Sussex). In between news cycles, they have found time to write on the secrets to a happy marriage and the pitfalls of the dating scene; the folly of heeding healthy eating advice and the absurdities of modern business-speak; the complications of online shopping, AI translation and getting overly familiar with Siri; and the popularity of *The Daily Telegraph* with the nation's poultry. The richness and variety of their experiences never fail to impress.

This is the 17th volume in the series of Unpublished Letters to the Editor. As ever, my thanks go to Richard Green and the team at Quarto; to Matt for his splendid cover cartoon; and to the Letters Editor, Orlando Bird, for keeping order throughout the year. Lastly, I would like to thank the letter-writers themselves. There is no wisdom quite like common sense, and no better antidote to intellectual pomposity than humour. Though they may not profess to be experts, our readers have an unrivalled capacity for mischief and merriment. Long may that continue.

Kate Moore
London SW1

FAMILY
TRIALS AND
TRIBULATIONS

A modest proposal

SIR – I was driving my girlfriend to friends for dinner when my hand accidentally touched her knee while changing gear. Oh dear, I said, I'll have to marry you now. OK, she replied. That was 55 years ago.

Peter Jordan
Pinner, Middlesex

SIR – In 1969 we were parked outside the nurses' home when my boyfriend asked me to marry him. My response was to say he would need to ask me on bended knee.

As it was raining outside he spent several minutes attempting to kneel in the driver's side well of a Mini car and proposed. I accepted immediately.

Patricia Ann Wilkins
Upminster, Essex

SIR – I proposed to my wife on the island of Anguilla, on a Saturday afternoon. There was no horse racing on the television, so it appealed as a quite an excellent idea.

Justin Tahany
Reading, Berkshire

SIR – Reading the stories about unusual proposals reminded me of the first conversation my wife and I had.

She was part way up a rock climb and used her knee to reach a ledge.

Use of knees is frowned upon in climbing circles, so I shouted "knees". She replied: "Bugger off."

I didn't and we've been married 47 years now.

Incidentally I now have two artificial knees and she still uses biological ones.

Geoff Vaughan
Warrington, Cheshire

SIR – I proposed to my future wife in the car park at Guildford Cathedral. However, I outdid this romantic venue one Valentine's Day; I took her to watch Scunthorpe United play at Accrington Stanley. We approach our 53rd wedding anniversary.

Rev Alan Wright
Barton upon Humber, North Lincolnshire

SIR – You report a trend whereby people are claiming that they are on honeymoon in order to get a hotel upgrade.

My wife and I occasionally experience the reverse situation, being allocated the honeymoon suite, unexpectedly and certainly without blagging.

I suspect it could have something to do with my name being misheard or misinterpreted during the booking process.

Alan Honeyman
Scarborough, North Yorkshire

No ill feelings

SIR – Valentine's Day. A day when there's a slight feeling of hope in the air. I hope that this year my husband may grab an actual Valentine's Day card off the shelf when he rushes into the village shop at the last minute and not, like last year, a Get Well Soon card.

Zanzie Griffin
Cullompton, Devon

SIR – As the annual love-heart and romance festival got under way, I wondered, as one does, what the ideal anti-Valentine meal might be. Perhaps kippers with Brussels sprouts and Stilton cheese sauce?

Tim Bradbury
Northwich, Cheshire

In it for the long haul

SIR – Sir James Dyson more than deserved a title for persevering with his belief in the first ever bagless vacuum. However, Lady Dyson should have been given an award for her endless patience. It took 5,127 prototypes before he succeeded. Most of us would have said after the 50th prototype: "Darling, is this really going to work?"

Tricia Barnes
Beaconsfield, Buckinghamshire

SIR – My advice for a happy marriage is never to forget your wedding anniversary.

Being an avid angler, and with this in mind, I set the wedding date for the start of the fishing season in June. The other advice, which I presented in my speech, was that if you give a man a fish, he would be fed for a day, but teach a man to fish, and you could get rid of him for the whole weekend.

After 52 years, I believe the latter advice to be the most important.

Alan Belk
Leatherhead, Surrey

SIR – There are two words that can lead to a long and happy marriage – "Yes Dear". I speak from experience.

John Harrison
Crawley, West Sussex

SIR – If only everyone was as fortunate as me. I have been married for over thirty years to a man who knows everything. Imagine that.

Deb Carroll
Stockport, Cheshire

SIR – I know I'm always right, I just pretend I'm not sure.

Jo E. Tanner
Deltona, Florida, United States

SIR – My late husband told me that he had a Running Away Fund and a Coming Back In Case It Doesn't Work Out Fund. We were very happy together but you can never be too careful, can you?

> **Rachel Palmer**
> Rhayader, Radnorshire

SIR – I thought the secret to a happy marriage was an amicable divorce, until I received the reply to a card I had sent my first wife congratulating her on our golden divorce anniversary.

> **Bruce Denness**
> Niton, Isle of Wight

SIR – My husband refers to me as his first wife. I introduce my husband as my last husband.

> **Barbara Speakman**
> Worlaby, North Lincolnshire

SIR – In the Ask an Expert column of your Money section your reader proposed divorcing his wife to marry her mother, allowing him to inherit the mother's estate on her death.

The financial adviser says it works but HMRC might seek to annul the marriage if it was unconsummated. Were I to propose this to my wife I think it might make for some awkward conversations at the dinner table.

> **D.H.F. Stabler**
> Cambridge

SIR – I recall waking up from my quadruple bypass operation at St George's Hospital, Tooting. I suddenly had a melancholy moment and said to the nurse, "I need to telephone my wife, I'm not sure I'm going to make it through the night."

A male orderly looked at me and said, "Call her now mate and you probably won't make it. It's two o'clock in the morning."

I didn't make the call.

William Freeman
East Molesey, Surrey

SIR – In listing the type of book he expects to see in the libraries of upholders of diversity, Michael Deacon includes a book whose pages are entirely blank. I have just such a book. The cover title is *All That Men Know About Women*. It is the Unabridged and Unexpurgated edition. A fascinating read it is, too.

William Fay
Sherfield-on-Loddon, Hampshire

Mother load

SIR – I am a great fan of Mother's Day. It always falls on a Sunday; I feel appreciated by my children and receive gifts, cards and flowers, but without the inconvenience of being a year older. This year, however, I felt rather cheated as the day coincided with my husband's birthday. As I'm sure you can appreciate, this caused us a few issues, such as who deserved to be the most spoiled on the day and who was going to cook the Sunday roast. I won't reveal who won out on the day, but after some research, I am relieved to see that these two important family events will not clash again until 2087 when I will be the grand age of 125.

Catherine Kidson
Bradfield, Berkshire

SIR – Some years ago the last of three verses on a Mother's Day card from my son (then aged six) read: "You're getting old, beginning to fold, so make this day 'Happy Mother's Day'".

Su Sainsbury
Sunbury on Thames, Surrey

All in the delivery

SIR – When my daughter was pregnant 16 years ago her husband told his boss which fortnight he would like off for his paternity leave.

His boss said: "I'm going on a fishing holiday that fortnight, would you like to come with me?"

He wasn't joking.

Peter Collings
Winchester, Hampshire

SIR – When I was born, my dad said I looked like a frog run over by a bus. Thankfully my looks improved as I grew.

Carla Stainke
Alness, Ross-shire

SIR – My birth took place at half-time during the Cup Final between Newcastle and Arsenal many years ago.

My mother had a wide range of interests and, after learning the sex of her baby, immediately inquired after the half-time score (It was 0–0, with Newcastle going on to win 1–0).

I'll let footballing buffs work out how old I am.

> **Helen Green**
> Aberporth, Ceredigion

SIR – Overheard in the golf clubhouse, some years ago now:

"John wasn't there for the birth, were you John?"

"Well we had a match against RAF Seletar that afternoon."

> **Wg Cdr Roger Lindley (retd)**
> Tetbury, Gloucestershire

SIR – There was no paternity leave applicable when my two daughters were born in the early 1990s but they were canny enough each to make their appearance on a Saturday.

> **Phillip Pennicott**
> London E18

SIR – I was born on Christmas Eve in 1956, the youngest of four boys.

After I was delivered, my father proudly announced to my brothers that they had a new brother for

Christmas. My eldest brother Terry, then aged ten, was less than impressed. "But I wanted a bloody train set!"

> **Dan Rafferty**
> Bath, Somerset

SIR – When our family doctor delivered me in 1940 he didn't charge as my parents had paid for the delivery of my three elder brothers.

He was ahead of the supermarkets with buy four, get one free.

> **Tony Manning**
> Barton-on-Sea, Hampshire

SIR – As a reward for safely delivering our first child I bought my wife a brand new, grey, Mini in 1961 for £400.

Without my knowledge she immediately drove it around the corner, with a piece of pink carpet, to have it resprayed to match.

> **Roger Collings**
> Presteigne, Radnorshire

As yet untitled

SIR – Parents need caution in the naming of offspring. When my wife was pregnant with our firstborn we discussed names. For a boy I quite fancied Russell until the obvious was pointed out.

> **Ray Cattle**
> Wateringbury, Kent

SIR – My father wanted to name me Hugh but my mother resisted, feeling I would be ridiculed at school.

David Ray
Norwich

SIR – My niece was named Piglet until the need to make a decision for her birth registration was imminent. She still answers to Piglet 28 years on.

Rosie Harden-Vane
Holywell, Northumberland

SIR – My son, who has a great interest in Polar exploration, named his daughter Megan Adelie. A son followed and we were greatly relieved when Alexander was given the second name Magellan. We had feared Emperor, Macaroni or even Chinstrap.

Sue Wagstaff
Via email

SIR – When my parents were living in Bermondsey in 1950 and my mother was pregnant with me and thinking about possible names, she happened to see a van bearing the legend "Maxwell's Bagwash Laundry".

I have always thought how fortunate I am that her eyes did not stray to the second word.

Maxwell Sawyer
Stamford, Lincolnshire

SIR – A friend's father decreed that all four of his children should have names beginning with the same letter, so that only one order of nametapes was necessary.

Simon Crewe
Plymouth, Devon

SIR – I am sure that my parents called me Michael so that underwear, shirts and trousers already had a sewn-in label.

My mother never edited the St. and I didn't live up to the prefix either.

Michael Marks
Leominster, Herefordshire

SIR – After a great deal of deliberation, we gave our daughter the middle name Augusta – after the golf course.

Rosalind Doye
London SW18

SIR – My granddaughter suggested her baby brother could be called John Lewis. He wasn't.

Janice Haynes
Cullompton, Devon

SIR – Andrew Carpenter, CEO of the Structural Timber Association, appears to have landed his dream job.

Alan Tomlinson
Cheadle, Cheshire

Small but mighty

SIR – When my daughter was three years old, I found her in the vegetable aisle of a supermarket telling a man what vegetables to buy. When I asked her what she was doing, he answered: "Getting training for her life's work, bossing men around."

She is now a compliance consultant.

Carole Oswin
Woodford Green, Essex

SIR – Our four-year-old granddaughter just said to me, "Grandpa, will you help me to find my bracelet?"

"When did you lose it?" I asked.

"About ten years ago," came the reply.

One wanted to laugh, but didn't.

Philip Everall
Crewe, Cheshire

SIR – In a prize draw at his local butcher in the run-up to Christmas, my adult son won a chicken. When I next saw my four-year-old grandson, I said in an excited voice that I'd heard his dad had won a chicken. "Yes," he replied with a seriousness that suggested he was not impressed, "but it was dead".

Peter Saunders
Cardiff

SIR – Going through my mother's affairs after her passing we found a cache of sayings and letters she'd received from her grandchildren over the years. From my seven-year-old son: "Dear Gran, thanks for the vultures, they will be very useful."

Heather Du Faur
Goring, Oxfordshire

How to be Topp

SIR – My granddaughter has written an essay all about the Abdominal Snowman. I didn't have the heart to tell her.

Ian Cribb
Poole, Dorset

SIR – A dyslexic pupil once wrote that her boyfriend had "huged her sweatly".

Before correcting her work, I remember – just for a moment – almost envying her ability to produce what appeared to be a wonderful parody of Chaucerian ribaldry.

Patrick Miller
Hartlepool, Co Durham

SIR – My younger brother was among the first cohort of pupils to be diagnosed with dyslexia, in the 1960s.

On being awarded a scholarship to Truro School, our Dutch mother, whose English was always uncertain, informed the headmaster that Paul had special needs as he was bisexual.

On close questioning after returning home she said both words had an x in them, hence the confusion.

Helen Keats
Brighstone, Isle of Wight

SIR – My grandson's school changed the theme for World Book Day to dressing as an adjective rather than a character from a book. A white fur Yeti costume had already been bought for my grandson, so he went as "furry".

A boy in his class wore a grey hoodie and grey trousers and went as "boring". Brilliant, I thought.

Maureen Bell
Gateshead, Tyne and Wear

SIR – My last school report from my Latin teacher read: "He sails around in an uncharted ocean". I managed to prove him wrong.

Captain Nairn Lawson MN (retd)
Portbury, Somerset

Stiff upper lip

SIR – My sister and I, growing up, never looked alike. But now we're in our seventies, friends say that we've started to resemble each other. Perhaps because we're both growing moustaches.

Julia Malone
Haslemere, Surrey

SIR – As a young National Service man in the RAF in Pakistan I grew a moustache to impress my girlfriend. I sent her a photograph of myself in a desert jacket and shorts with my new facial decoration. By way of a response, I received a Valentine card. Sadly it contained no handwritten words of affection. Sewn into the card was a razor blade.

Peter Dawson
Nottingham

SIR – I used to get a very sore upper lip after shaving when I was a student at Guy's Hospital. I went to the doctor to ask if he could give me some ointment to ease the soreness.

His reply was succinct. "Stop shaving it, you bloody idiot!"

I have had a moustache ever since.

Dr Steve Cowling
Via email

Still ticking over

SIR – You report that people approaching retirement will be given a health MOT. As I am in that position I would much rather have a service to keep me going, rather than an MOT, as I'm not sure what would happen if I failed it.

Dr A.J.J. Bentley
Houghton on the Hill, Leicestershire

SIR – Richard Coles, aged 63, says his favourite age was 38. My father chose to remain at 38 until he died aged 80.

Mark Solon
London EC3

SIR – I know of a former employee of a chain of supermarkets who was given a final warning for not demanding proof of age when a customer bought alcohol. His defence that he had asked the customer for proof the previous week and had assumed he had not got any younger in the intervening week was not accepted.

Jeremy Douglas-Jones
Swansea

SIR – We were in Yosemite National Park around 20 years ago. I popped into the general store leaving my ID in the car, assuming I wouldn't need it to buy a couple of beers. At the till, sure enough I was challenged. Being in my early thirties and already significantly balding I lifted my cap, smiled and asked "Will this do?" as I tipped my head forward. Not a flicker of amusement from the cashier. Needless to say, I returned to my car with my tail between my legs to fetch my passport.

Anthony Dyer
Cambridge

SIR – Should I seek compensation or open some champagne, having been called "babe" at the age of 69?

Anthony Ireson
Windley, Derbyshire

Creature comforts

SIR – You report the rise of the "human dog bed". I have noticed a growing trend for children to be dressed as animals (woolly hats with bear ears) and animals to be dressed as humans (hats, coats, leggings). I suppose common sleeping arrangements were inevitable.

Maggie Rayner
Neston, Wiltshire

SIR – If, as recommended by the action group Climate Cymru BAME, anti-racist dog-free zones are created in rural Wales, can my dog be exempt from exclusion? He is a border collie and, being both black and white, clearly is not a racist dog.

David Vincent
Cranbrook, Kent

SIR – Oops, I missed International Cat Day, August 8 – but it's OK as my cat has declared that every day is cat day.

Dennis Fitzgerald
Melbourne, Australia

SIR – My cat, Freddie, decided he would bypass
the professionals when he was looking for
accommodation. He walked into my house, gave it a
thorough inspection and decided it would suit him.
It has been run to his exacting standards for the last
eight years.

Dorothy Jameson
Barnard Castle, Co Durham

SIR – As I type this, Tiddles and Blackie – the two
fluffy cats living across the stream from me – are
feigning squaring up to each other on the big wooden
fence. They have moved past the hunched shoulders
and screwy neck phase and have proceeded to the
feline motorcycle noises phase.

At any moment, there will be a pause to look back
and see if their staff are about to run out from their
kitchens with fresh yummies, or whether their efforts
to bag a second breakfast from panicking stepparents
desperate to distract their fur babies from coming to
blows have been in vain.

Thank God cats don't have access to nuclear
weapons – their love of brinkmanship with humanity
is truly terrifying.

Mark Boyle
Johnstone, Renfrewshire

SIR – As if things could get no worse in this mad
world in which I now live, my year-old Jack Russell
puppy ate my new NHS hearing aids.

What really annoys me is not the minimal cost of replacing them, but that it would appear the dog still cannot hear me, even when I shout at him.

Yours in silence,

Simon Perks
Poughill, Devon

Wrong day to diet

SIR – Your article on the dangers of veganism made depressing reading for cannibals and tigers. Not only do they have to spend hours tracking and catching their human prey, but now they have to expend vital energy struggling to identify the right kind of human to eat, namely, one with all the appropriate proteins and minerals. "Eat up your vegan!" just won't wash anymore when you're trying to get the kids – or cubs – to stay strong and healthy.

Andreas Smith
Bishop Auckland, Co Durham

SIR – Your article about the dangers of going vegan misses the greatest danger of them all.

Upon becoming vegan, 100 per cent of people become utterly crushing bores and develop an inability to walk into any room without loudly announcing their dietary choices.

A terrible fate for all who convert.

Andrew Pearce
London SE3

SIR – Lest some of the healthy eating advice put forward in a number of your articles cause undue anxiety, fellow readers may like to note that not eating is an unwise long-term health strategy.

> **W.H.L.**
> Via email

SIR – In the same week that the vibrant Shrewsbury Market Hall won the title of Britain's favourite market (for the third year in a row), the *Telegraph*'s NHS tracker ranked the Shrewsbury and Telford Hospital NHS Trust the worst hospital in England based on average A&E, cancer and appointment waiting times.

Perhaps access to delicious artisan sourdough is inversely proportional to efficiency and performance of the local healthcare service?

> **Tim Cozze-Young**
> Shrewsbury, Shropshire

SIR – The rise in popularity of sourdough stems from people filling their time during lockdown by baking the stuff. I found sitting in the park with a good bottle of wine and *The Daily Telegraph* to be a much better use of my time.

> **Julian Badenoch**
> Cowes, Isle of Wight

SIR – As a competent left-handed bread slicer, I moaned about the right-handed members of my household who were incapable of slicing evenly. I should have had more sense. They've taken the hint and have deserted the kitchen permanently, leaving each and every culinary struggle to me.

Joanna Whatley
Charing, Kent

SIR – The only way to improve a fruit salad is to lock it safely in a time capsule and send it back to the 1970s where it belongs.

Sam Kendall-Marsden
Huntingdon, Cambridgeshire

SIR – In light of their simple and logical solution to the longstanding problem of how to extract the last of the beans from the can, should Heinz representatives be invited to take part in the Middle East peace talks?

Geoff Johnson
Gateshead, Tyne and Wear

SIR – If the human race is incapable of removing baked beans from the tin, should they really be allowed out?

Sue Mason
Spalding, Lincolnshire

No accounting for tastes

SIR – Some years ago when my children were teenagers we had two French exchange students staying with us for a week. One evening I decided to cook a typical British meal for them and chose toad in the hole. Unfortunately they took the name of the dish literally and refused to eat it. No amount of explaining that it was sausages in a batter and not actual toads would make them try it.

Matty Thacker
Tanworth in Arden, Warwickshire

SIR – While staying with my wife and young daughters at a west London hotel we watched a Japanese gentleman help himself to a selection from the breakfast bar of scrambled egg, sausage, black pudding and bacon. Coming to the final dish, he took the top off, looked quizzically at the contents and helped himself to a generous dollop of porridge.

It looked perfectly fine to me and I'm sure he enjoyed it.

Julian Gallimore
Hereford

SIR – Back in the 1990s when my late wife, Judy, worked for Saga Holidays, it was company policy to ensure that their customers staying in Spanish hotels over Christmas enjoyed a traditional Christmas lunch. Resort reps were sent out laden with Christmas puddings. One hotel wasn't sure what to do with them so served them with gravy.

Christopher Ainsworth
Bodmin, Cornwall

SIR – Cousin's 21st.
Darkened grain store lined with colourful material.
Long buffet table.
Lobster and brandy butter.
Never again!

Michael Cleary
York

Critical drinking

SIR – The moves by the Government towards shutting pubs once and for all are to be welcomed. On the rare occasions I have visited a pub recently, I have seen people gather together in groups of three or more, imbibe strong drink, and actually criticise our Government, often in quite memorable terms.

This last point is important, since the recipients of such comments often remember them, and repeat them to their friends.

Any governing party would obviously want to stop such practices and keep people at home, watching programmes on TV, which show the Government in a better light.

The lockdown couldn't work indefinitely, so maybe shutting pubs will do the trick.

Andrew Puckett
Taunton, Somerset

SIR – When I was running a pub in Moreton-in-Marsh a well-dressed gentleman walked up to the bar one Saturday lunchtime and – quite loudly – asked the barman: "May I bring in a well-behaved bitch?"

On being given consent he returned ten minutes later followed by an equally elegant lady and – to the relief of all – a clearly female pedigree golden retriever.

Christopher Horne
Rickmansworth, Hertfordshire

SIR – A friend of my brother-in-law was given a half pint of beer when he asked for a drink. He held it up and said: "What am I supposed to do with this, lick it?"

Jean Macdonald
Hayling Island, Hampshire

SIR – Could somebody please brew a beer and call it "Responsibly": then I can drink as much as I want.

Geoff Evans
Trewellard, Cornwall

SIR – As a very junior dental house officer at Guy's Hospital in 1969, I was responsible for a lady who had fallen in the street nearby and had her jaws wired together for stability.

On her recovery from the anaesthetic, I enquired whether she drank Guinness, as I was allowed to prescribe her a bottle morning and evening.

Her instant reply was: "Is that all?"

We then speculated on the reason for her fall.

> **Chris Cox**
> Canterbury, Kent

SIR – I started my university degree as a ten and a half stone weakling. I finished four years later as an eleven and a half stone weakling. Guinness was available in the university bar.

> **Tony Scofield**
> Glastonbury, Somerset

SIR – When I was a thirtysomething lecturer I self-prescribed a daily bottle of Veuve Clicquot. May I recommend this remedy to everyone who must teach Classical languages to the young? It makes explaining Greek syntax so much more bearable.

> **Neil Sewell-Rutter**
> Oxford

SIR – Recent letters about Pimm's reminded me of the occasion when my father-in-law, then a sprightly, independent nonagenarian, accepted an invitation to the wedding of a relative of an elderly friend. He lived on the edge of Dartmoor and travelled into Tavistock by bus for the event.

When we later asked him how he enjoyed it, this lifelong teetotaller replied that he had had a lovely time, and they provided a delicious fruit cup to drink.

He did, however, say that someone must have put him on the bus afterwards as he didn't remember getting home.

Susan Price
Bingham, Nottinghamshire

Clothes maketh the man

SIR – While I applaud the advice that dips provide an outstanding upper body workout for men in their sixties, I am disturbed by the implication that gentlemen in their sixties might be wearing T-shirts in public to show off the results. This seriously undermines two decades of effort on my part to encourage my son to wear a shirt with a collar. Work in progress.

Ian Thompson
Ingst, South Gloucestershire

SIR – Can your sartorial correspondent reviewing men's overcoats reveal where his welcomed return of "respectable" male attire after its hiatus of the past 50 years is to be seen?

Richard Lennox
Langholm, Dumfriesshire

SIR – I'm quite jealous of Tom Tugendhat and his 60 or 70 pairs of green socks. I thought I was doing well with my 50 pairs of burgundy socks.

Rob Dorrell
Bath, Somerset

SIR – The only place to see thigh-length boots are on a good-looking woman. I can already hear the cries of anguish from some of my sisterhood. I'll get my coat.

Cherry Tugby
Warminster, Wiltshire

SIR – After completing a horseback ride across Scotland I took the family for a celebratory dinner at a smart hotel. The maître d', resplendent in kilt, said: "Do we have a jacket sir?"

It is a matter of lifelong regret that I did not reply: "Do we have any trousers?"

Bill Knight
London N5

SIR – An eccentric member of a local golf club was asked to leave the club lounge as he was not wearing a jacket and tie.

He re-appeared a few minutes later wearing a jacket, tie and underpants – but nothing else.

Luke Grant
Pensax Common, Worcestershire

SIR – Yesterday we went out to lunch with friends; he came downstairs wearing moleskin trousers.

I said, "Bit warm for those, isn't it?" He changed into corduroys.

I could always spot him on a crowded beach too as he was in long trousers. Shorts are for Greek holidays only.

Amanda Gunn
Hereford

SIR – I think I'll pass on flares this time around. In the 1970s I was on a government course in London and having a lunchtime bite to eat in a pub on Shaftesbury Avenue. I was feeling very daring and cosmopolitan in my new flares, when the late Danny La Rue and friends came in from a theatre opposite. Looking me up and down, he remarked: "Well hello, Sailor!" They all collapsed, as did my resolve to wear them any further.

Colin Drury
Dinas Powys, Glamorgan

Water, water everywhere

SIR – Water found on Mars! Please do not let Thames Water anywhere near it.

Graeme Brierley
Sutton Bridge, Lincolnshire

SIR – I read that Thames Water is described as a "troubled water" company.

Perhaps it is in need of a bridge.

Jane Moth
Stone, Staffordshire

Not on the high street

SIR – In the lovely days of department stores I was being served by an assistant when a man asked her if she had any fallopian tubes. She replied in the affirmative. "Well how much are they?" She said that hers were not for sale as she would rather keep them. Light began to dawn.

"Oh lord, what have I asked for!"

"Fluorescent tubes perhaps?"

"That's the one."

"Lighting department, first floor."

Marilyn Morgan
Southsea, Hampshire

SIR – The lady at the hardware counter looked totally blank when I said I was looking for a violin … to cut vegetables.

Isabel Page
Oldmeldrum, Aberdeenshire

SIR – My wife has just been searching online for a *Telegraph* Sudoku book. She found several reduced price "used" books. We thought these might not be quite as difficult to solve as unused puzzle books.

Geoffrey Clark
Swindon, Wiltshire

SIR – My wife purchased a new hairdryer online yesterday. It arrived this morning – a good make, but upon unpacking it there was some confusion. After she had read the instructions, there was a warning: THIS ITEM CONTAINS NUTS.

Ian Duckworth
Billington, Lancashire

SIR – I recently bought a lightweight showerproof jacket from M&S. The washing instructions included: "cool tumble with several tennis balls". Game, set and match!

Joyce Bentley
Stafford

SIR – The turn buttons that keep the door on my shed shut are going rusty. I wanted to see if Google Lens could recommend the best place to get new ones. Here is what Google AI said about it when I submitted a photograph:

"The item appears to be an old, possibly antique, jade pendant, potentially from the Liangzhu culture in China. It's carved with a 'San Cha Xing Qi' design and has a visible, possibly unintentional, Phillips head screw imprint."

If anyone would like "an old possibly antique jade pendant, possibly from the Liangzhu culture in China", I can supply them. And since new ones cost around £3 per pair from B&Q or Amazon, I'm sure I'll have an almost endless supply. Going cheap!

David Chantrey
Bridgnorth, Shropshire

Shop til you drop

SIR – I understand that Amazon is now trialling the use of drones to drop customers' orders onto their premises.

Perhaps I should have second thoughts about ordering that bone china dinner set.

John W. Smith
Gloucester

SIR – The parcel delivery firm Evri has sent me a text to inform me that it couldn't deliver a package and gave me an address and map reference where I could collect it. Unfortunately the address is in Mountain View, a suburb of San Francisco.

David Simkins
Lower Stondon, Bedfordshire

SIR – It is reported that Smithfield meat market is going to close after 800 years. As a Freeman of the City of London, I am entitled to drive a flock of sheep across London Bridge to Smithfield free of tax. What am I to do if Smithfield is moved to Deptford, as is predicted? My sheep will arrive exhausted and so will I.

Sandy Pratt
Storrington, West Sussex

I vow to thee my county

SIR – I am pleased to have two children. They were both born in the same room of the (then) Royal Victoria Hospital Boscombe, Bournemouth. The elder, Katherine, was born in Hampshire, and the younger, James, was born in Dorset.

They have argued the merits of each county ever since.

Malcolm Freeth
Bournemouth, Dorset

SIR – In April 1974 I had half of a bacon and egg pie for supper and went to sleep under a continental quilt in Warwickshire.

I woke the next morning beneath a duvet in the West Midlands and ate the remainder of last night's Quiche Lorraine for my breakfast.

Mark Carver-Smith
Barwell, Leicestershire

SIR – Spare a thought for us Lancastrians saddled with Merseyside. The Beatles got out just in time.

Alex Robb
Liverpool

Heart in the right place

SIR – Having come back to live in Ireland after more than a decade in the UK, I knew that I was "home" when I saw a sign on the door of a curtains and blinds shop: "Blind Repairs".

Jane Fleming
New Ross, Co Wexford, Ireland

SIR – The residents of Ashlar Village living in roads with weird medical resonances can be grateful the estate wasn't built on the site of a disused sewage treatment plant.

Brian Inns
Melksham, Wiltshire

SIR – All credit to Glasgow City Council for trying to preserve the memory of an old hospital with street names, but Mortuary Close might take some effort to sell.

Lovat Timbrell
Brighton, East Sussex

SIR – My wife's former employer lived next to a cemetery at the end of a cul-de-sac. His wife vetoed his suggestion that the house be named "Dead End".

Peter Nokes
Sittingbourne, Kent

Grave concerns

SIR – I received this morning a letter in the post with "This Spring, treat yourself on us" printed on the envelope. I didn't open it, as also printed on the envelope was "Pure Cremation".

Geoff Riley
Saffron Walden, Essex

SIR – Checking through the small print in the contract for my prepaid cremation-only plan, I came across a clause that guarantees a 50 per cent refund of the monies paid, if I should die in a fire.

Bob Readman
Sevenoaks, Kent

SIR – When my mother died in 1990, I was responsible for notifying relevant people of her death. I naturally contacted her bank. To my surprise, a week or two later, l received a letter addressed to Mrs Rushworth (deceased). On opening l found that it started off "Dear Mrs Rushworth (deceased)".

I was very tempted to return it as "forwarding address unknown".

Hilary Young
Hadleigh, Suffolk

SIR – When my father died unexpectedly, my mother turned to me and said: "That's lucky, I bought a new black coat last week."

Timothy Morgan-Owen
Melbourne, Derbyshire

SIR – I was interested to read about the large asteroid crashing to Earth on December 22, 2032. As I will then be 86 years of age, I would like to visit the expected site at 05:25. This would save me all the inconvenience and cost of my old age and the death certificate would impress my descendant: "Hit by asteroid".

David Faulks
Hove, East Sussex

SIR – Following the news that cemeteries are becoming full and the proposition that after 75 years burials could be in old graves, I would like to put my name down for a plot in Westminster Abbey.

Dr Paddy Fielder
Woodbridge, Suffolk

SIR – When a well-known village character (a well-proportioned ex landlord of a village pub) sadly passed away a few years ago his funeral took place in one of the local churches. With the church full to bursting the coffin was wheeled in through a side door, and to everyone's amusement a sign at the end of the coffin read: "Wide Load". This certainly lightened the mood of all present and gave him a good send-off.

Rosemary Ridge
Rowlands Castle, Hampshire

SIR – The recent comments on funerals reminded me of a family discussion about burial or cremation.

I was kindly told: "You couldn't be buried, you're claustrophobic."

How thoughtful!

Ann Sunley
Uttoxeter, Staffordshire

SIR – I have told my family not to waste money on a coffin at my funeral. As I have been around trucks and transport all my working life, just put me on a pallet and shrink-wrap me.

Steve Cartridge
Bolton, Lancashire

The grand finale

SIR – I've asked that "Waltzing Matilda" be played as my coffin enters the church. Apparently a band was playing it in the street while I was being conceived and it seems appropriate to have it at both ends.

Maggie Hughes
Gnosall, Staffordshire

SIR – I have asked for "Hi Ho Silver Lining" (Jeff Beck) as I depart through the crematorium curtains. If my arm doesn't come out of the coffin and punch the sky, I am truly dead.

Graham Sharp
Market Drayton, Shropshire

SIR – As an avid Elvis fan I would like "Return to Sender" played at my funeral.

Harriet Robinson
Chillerton, Isle of Wight

SIR – Knowing that some of my acquaintances will be anxious to get at the wine and pork pies, I have chosen my favourite piece of music to be played at my funeral. It is Verdi's *Requiem*. A beautiful piece which lasts about 80 minutes.

Chris Ryder
Cheadle, Cheshire

To Siri with love

SIR – My husband always thanks Siri when, having mislaid his phone, he calls out, "Hey Siri where are you?" and Siri replies, "I'm over here".

He also likes to tell Siri how kind she is for setting our morning alarm on his phone. Siri answers "You're welcome", and the compliments go back and forth a few more times.

I once caught him asking Siri if she knew it was his birthday.

I'm glad he has someone else to talk to; it lets me off the hook.

Judy Parsley
London W4

SIR – As I approach old age I am beginning to wonder if I will need an app to get into heaven. If I do, no doubt I would have forgotten the password.

Richard Anderson
Winchester, Hampshire

SIR – You report that Russia hacked Sir Keir Starmer's "dangerously obvious" email account.

"Incorrect" is a helpful password to choose. Whenever you forget, or enter it incorrectly, the PC reminds you: "Your password is incorrect".

Dr Robert Bruce-Chwatt
Richmond, Surrey

SIR – I'm wondering exactly what information the Chinese are hoping to gain from the air fryer in my kitchen. It's either my secret spiced parsnip soup recipe or the new method I'm using to make mince pies. Whatever it is, I'm not revealing the recipe out loud just in case.

Georgia Moore
Nottingham

SIR – The last time my gas boiler was serviced British Gas installed a monitor on a high wall in the corner of the kitchen. Whenever any interesting cooking was in progress it shrieked and was very difficult to access and silence. It has now been demoted to a low shelf so at the first peep it can be removed to the naughty step outside the kitchen and the kitchen door firmly closed on it. That should teach it!

Bob Paterson
Oxted, Surrey

Life, the universe and everything

SIR – The report that exoplanet K2-18b appears to have an atmosphere that indicates that there are living organisms, such as marine phytoplankton, puts one in mind of *The Hitchhiker's Guide to the Galaxy*. That book revealed that the Earth was governed by dolphins. Perhaps it is time that Ed Miliband replaced his use of private jets with a canoe and began communing with them.

Richard Coulson
Gillingham, Kent

SIR – The pointless 11-minute Blue Origin space flight brought a wonderful response from my wife: "I spent longer than that on Space Mountain in Disney World".

Tony Ellison
Westcliff-on-Sea, Essex

SIR – Scientists seeking a suitable environment for recreated woolly mammoths need to think laterally. If they were kept at mouse size, it would be much easier to find suitable locations. Holes in the skirting boards might become a problem, though.

J. Drakeford
Arundel, West Sussex

Hold the phone

SIR – While considering our retirement plans, my wife and I often gaze longingly through the coastal properties in your Saturday Home section. However, our musings are always abruptly checked when we remind ourselves that such a move would necessarily involve trying to contact BT.

Pete Lynch Williams
Malvern, Worcestershire

From pillarbox to post

SIR – If first-class post has a 90 per cent chance of next day delivery, and second-class post with an alternate day service has a 95 per cent chance of delivery within three days, what is the optimum time for despatch to ensure a birthday card arrives on the recipient's birthday?

Answers on a postcard, and please show your workings. I suspect the solution is to deliver it yourself.

Peter Roberts
Crickhowell, Brecknockshire

SIR – What do I do now that my supply of large elastic bands has run out, given that the postman no longer drops them on the path?

Eileen Harrington
Doncaster

Look after the pennies

SIR – I read with horror the argument for copper coinage to be withdrawn. Apart from the nostalgic and linguistic gaps this will leave in our lives, how on earth am I going to keep my tulips upright in their vases?

Nicole Smith
Kew, Surrey

SIR – For those readers who are happy to see the removal of our copper coinage or see them as an inconvenience, I am happy to provide a free disposal service.

Sam Baxter
Fincham, Norfolk

My eyes are up here

SIR – Your article reports that fashion seems to be encouraging women to display large stretches of their cleavage, but since we men are not allowed to look or comment, may I suggest the reintroduction of the codpiece? This may level the playing field, since any feminine glance to such a low level would be obvious.

> **Ian Brent-Smith**
> Bicester, Oxfordshire

SIR – When I was a young girl we all wore stilettos. If a young man became too fresh a small jab with the heel on the toe of his shoe soon sorted the problem out.

> **Diane Baines**
> Sutton, Surrey

SIR – My father attempted to hide his copy of *Lady Chatterley's Lover* from my mother in plain sight by putting it on the bookshelf with the spine turned inwards, where it rapidly attracted my teenage curiosity.

My school satchel was a far better hiding place.

> **Sue McMillan**
> Hampton, Middlesex

SIR – Keen to find out what all the fuss was about, my late spinster great aunt Ada purchased a copy of *Lady Chatterley's Lover*. Knowing that her spinster sister Emily, with whom she lived, would disapprove, she put the book into the dust jacket of *Mr Middleton's Garden Book* and sat reading it by the fire.

Kate Forrester
Malvern, Worcestershire

Believe it or not

SIR – My late mother, whose parents hailed from Lewis, always observed the Sabbath, a tradition embedded in me for many years. However, in my thirties temptation came my way and I hung the washing out one Sunday, unaware that I had left my wristwatch in the pocket of the trousers to be washed. It never worked again. God moves in mysterious ways.

Catherine Porter
Crayke, North Yorkshire

SIR – I have the greatest sympathy for those poor souls suffering from the cold while attending divine worship.

With falling congregations, the Church of England should not lose sight of the fact that there is a business rival who can offer extreme heat for eternity at minimal cost.

Nicholas Young
London W13

SIR – At my Catholic primary school in the 1950s, when we were being taught about the commandment "Thou shalt not steal", we were told that stealing more than £5 was a mortal sin.

I wonder what the going rate is today?

Mike Fowler
Princes Risborough, Buckinghamshire

SIR – Perhaps our next Archbishop of Canterbury could be a Christian who believes in God?

Joe Greaves
Fleckney, Leicestershire

SIR – It is a truth universally acknowledged that the Church of England finds itself in something of a moral and numerical decline. Various reasons have been suggested, including secularism, social change and a loss of conviction, but I propose an overlooked yet obvious culprit: the clerical collar.

Once a firm symbol of spiritual authority, the so-called dog collar has remained stubbornly unchanged, while actual dog restraints have evolved considerably. Modern dogs now sport harnesses with multiple points of control, ergonomic fittings, and even GPS tracking. Meanwhile, our vicars persist with a single, rigid band, entirely out of step with contemporary canine best practice.

Could this sartorial stagnation be a metaphor for the Church's wider failure to adapt? Might a switch to something more in line with modern dog-walking technology, perhaps a brightly coloured, reinforced harness with reflective strips, or even one of those retractable devices, restore both moral authority and congregational discipline?

At the very least, it would make it easier to rein in errant bishops.

Ronald Lansdell
St Helier, Jersey

The Pope is a Catholic

SIR – Why should the 132 Cardinals of the Catholic Curia bother to go through the arcane and tedious ritual of voting for a new Pope when there is only one choice: Ralph Fiennes or Stanley Tucci?

Paul Strong
Claxby, Lincolnshire

SIR – Presumably Cardinal Pierbattista Pizzaballa will have no problem choosing his official name, if he is elected: Pope Domino.

Tim Johnson
Sawbridgeworth, Hertfordshire

SIR – Robert Prevost is our new Pope. He is to be known as Pope Leo XIV.
Personally, I would have preferred Pope Bob I.

Phil Angell
Helston, Cornwall

SIR – My dud hearing aid sprung into life when the new Pope was announced. Is this divine intearvention?

S. McVey
Deal, Kent

SIR – I suppose it really is a sign that you are getting on a bit when even the popes start to look young.

Kevin Richardson
London SE13

It never rains but it pours

SIR – During Storm Éowyn the roof of a cheese factory at Alpraham, Cheshire blew off.

There was De Brie everywhere! We all had to drive Caerphilly.

Tess Tavernor
Tarporley, Cheshire

SIR – Isn't it about time that someone informed the Met Office that it is fashionable nowadays to enjoy a Dry January?

Nigel Dickinson
High Wycombe, Buckinghamshire

SIR – Am I the only one disappointed by all the recent yellow snow warnings? It was definitely white.

Janette Weekes
Kilsby, Northamptonshire

SIR – "Here Comes the Sun" by Steve Harley & Cockney Rebel has been whizzing around my head since last Friday.

I'm not complaining as since last October it's been "It's Raining Again" by Supertramp.

Joanna Bunkham
Newton, Glamorgan

SIR – To counter the drought years, 18 months ago I started to conserve water around the house and collect jugs to water outdoor pots.

It hasn't stopped raining since.

Tomorrow I'm going to halt water collection and everyone can thank me when the sun comes out and stays out.

Lillie Roberts
Maidenhead, Berkshire

Dear North,

As part of the country's levelling-up agenda, please may we have some of your rain?

Yours,

The South
(Alan Brown
Medstead, Hampshire)

SIR – Thank goodness for the last two bank holidays; without them we would have a hosepipe ban by now.

David Brown
Preston, Lancashire

SIR – Those of a certain age will remember the heatwave and drought of 1976, and the exhortation to "Bathe with a friend". When we were young it was a wonderfully intimate thing to do, and officially encouraged as well.

Now with another water shortage and now we're of a certain age, at least we can help each other to get in and out of the bath.

Christopher Sharp
Kenilworth, Warwickshire

Pigeon English

SIR – When a pigeon cooed in our garden, my father would turn to my mother and say "He's right" – because he insisted the pigeon was saying "You DO look pretty".

When a pigeon says that to me, I always say "Thank you".

Carolyn Seabrook
Odiham, Hampshire

SIR – Chaffinches continue to remind me of my late mother-in-law who found the "Chop Suey Birds" quite irritating.

Dr Andy Ashworth
Bo'ness, West Lothian

SIR – There is a pigeon, now named Vivaldi, who persistently and accurately sings the first four notes of *Autumn* every morning.

I don't know whether it's his earworm, but it's certainly mine now.

Gillian Mitsi
Chalkida, Euboea, Greece

SIR – We recently celebrated Candlemas, when Joseph and Mary presented their young son at the Temple, and, as was tradition, upon arrival sacrificed two young pigeons.

Looking out at my garden today, and seeing the flattened state of my recently sprung daffodils, it occurred to me that this is a tradition which the new Archbishop of Canterbury, whoever he or she may be, must immediately reinstate.

Michael Latham
Oakham, Rutland

Voyage of the lawn treader

SIR – Our neighbours, who are on holiday in Italy, received a call from their robotic mower saying it had got stuck somewhere in the garden. Another neighbour had to go in and rescue it.

Duncan Rayner
Sunningdale, Berkshire

SIR – Many years ago a friend was mowing his lawn when he accidentally mowed over the family's tortoise. After that, Henry had a flat roof. He didn't suffer at all and lived for many years after the accident.

Rosemary Reed
Woodhall Spa, Lincolnshire

SIR – A recent survey has shown most people think dandelions, buttercups and daisies are weeds. They are correct. I know this because despite my being a gardener for over 50 years, they are the only things that, come rain or shine, thrive in my garden.

Martin Henry
Good Easter, Essex

SIR – With the Chelsea Flower Show unfolding, I thought your readers might be interested in the vase of flowers I have on my garden table. Bright and cheery, they have thrived for over a year through rain, wind, frost, and hail. My tip: buy plastic.

Ken McAdam
London W13

SIR – Monty Don's "dog-friendly" garden for the Chelsea Flower Show lacked one essential item: a lamp post.

Margaret Goslett
Richmond, Surrey

To everything there is a season

SIR – I have just purchased a rather nice summer outfit.

My husband has reliably informed me that my purchase shall ensure the end of summer and the onset of autumn.

Claire McCombie
Woodbridge, Suffolk

SIR – Joe Shute says, "This late stage of summer brings an unavoidable sense of melancholy; the darkening nights and damper mornings a reminder of something coming to an end."

On the contrary; it indicates that rugby, partridge and pheasant seasons are not far off.

George Adams
Brading, Isle of Wight

SIR – As I struggle to spell circadian rhythms correctly, spare a thought for Ethel, our Norfolk terrier, who really doesn't understand why breakfast is an hour later.

Tony Parrack
London SW20

SIR – Your editorial asks what we might do if we were to ever have a real winter again. I suggest that, looking back at various events over the past few years, we'd probably manage to get it all wrong.

David Costigan
Gosport, Hampshire

A YEAR IN POLITICS

Word of honour

SIR – The actor Stephen Mangan has said he would refuse an honour if it were offered to him. I once read a headline that said: "I will not be giving £1m to the university, says leading businessman."

For the avoidance of doubt, I will not be playing for Wales in the upcoming Six Nations.

Shimon Cohen
London N2

SIR – Given his woeful record as Mayor of London, I would recommend Sir Sadiq Khan as the first recipient of an entirely new honour for failed politicians – the Medal for Unrivalled Political Posturing and Empty Thinking. In time, the medal's acronym will catch on with the public.

The quality of Labour's Cabinet guarantees a rich flow of future nominees.

Fred Fearn
Bridport, Dorset

The hansom cabinet

SIR – A Londoner born and bred, I have used hundreds of black cabs and shared wonderful conversations with their incredible and well-informed drivers. I have long held the belief that we should fire all our useless politicians and install a consortium of black cab drivers instead. They would sort this nation out. I am sure they would welcome the opportunity.

Mary Hayter
Ledbury, Herefordshire

SIR – It strikes me that the world would be commensurately better off if all political leaders were replaced by comedians – it's working well in Ukraine.

Lance Warrington
Cirencester, Gloucestershire

SIR – Where are the grownups in this Government? It's rather like looking at a group of fifth formers struggling to run a village fete. With the exception of David Lammy. He hasn't even got out of the third form yet.

David Chamberlain
Houghton on the Hill, Leicestershire

SIR – Having observed Sir Ed Davey's exuberance in the run-up to the general election and comparing it with his current lacklustre performance in the Commons, surely it must be in the best interests of democracy to construct a soft play area in front of the Speaker's desk for his sole use.

Tony Hines
Market Rasen, Lincolnshire

SIR – It is indeed interesting that Boris Johnson likens himself to Cnut.

However I am not sure he has spelled it correctly.

Iain McAvoy
Findon, West Sussex

SIR – Whenever I read that Alastair Campbell has opined on any subject, I am seized with the grim sensation that will be familiar to anyone who has thrown a party and is wondering, long after midnight, when that last, barnacle-like guest will finally do the decent thing and go home.

Kevin Duffy
Manchester

SIR – You printed a prominent headline in Saturday's paper: "Farage: I could be Prime Minister before Trump leaves office".

I hate to be a party pooper, but so could I.

John Thompson
York

SIR – There is no conceivable question to which Nigel Farage is the correct answer.

Dr Rowan Hardy
Marshfield, Wiltshire

Political animals

SIR – Larry the cat has just risen further in my estimation following his reported refusals to pose for gratuitous photos with the Government.

H. Gelder
Rugby, Warwickshire

SIR – Possibly Larry was put off from offering the paw of friendship to Ian Murray, the Scottish Secretary, by the unappealing sight of his unpolished shoes?

Jill Morris
London W4

SIR – Apparently, no one is to be spared disappointment under this Government, not even Sir Keir Starmer's children. They've been given a cat, although they really wanted a dog,

Marie-Louise Neill
Battle, East Sussex

Change is afoot

SIR – Keir Starmer fought the last election on the mantra of change. He has been proved to be correct. However, we all thought it was going to be change for the better.

Neville Dickinson
Morpeth, Northumberland

SIR – Sir Keir Starmer has said that it will get worse before it gets better and it is true. After 25 years of a Labour government in Wales we have experience of this already. However, we are still waiting for it to get better.

Trevor Gall
Carmarthen

SIR – As Labour try to improve their image after a disastrous start in office, the Prime Minister rather naively says that the machinery of government is like turning an oil tanker.

That's great news – to turn an oil tanker going at full speed takes about four and a half minutes.

Neil Stuart
Tavistock, Devon

SIR – A short period of socialism is probably a good thing for the constitution as it will build up immunity for the future. However, a four-year spell seems a bit excessive.

Chris Davies
Woking, Surrey

Looking on the glum side

SIR – "Starmer downbeat in New Year message". Is that in contention for the title of least surprising headline ever?

David Harris
London SW13

SIR – Sir Keir Starmer is providing the nation with as much drama as Boris Johnson did, but without the optimism.

Andrew White
Alresford, Hampshire

SIR – They say all political careers eventually end in failure. Sir Keir Starmer seems to be in a hurry, however.

Christopher Hunt
Swanley, Kent

SIR – It seems that every time the Prime Minister steps outside No 10 he treads on a banana skin. Isn't there anyone in the Labour Party who can sweep the pavement beforehand?

Felicity Ogilvy
Bruton, Somerset

SIR – Always one to look for positives, I can happily say that Keir Starmer makes John Major look competent and charismatic.

Bob Massingham
Bicester, Oxfordshire

SIR – I have written to Father Christmas and asked for a new Prime Minister. I don't believe in Father Christmas any more, but who else is there to turn to?

Wendy May
Hereford

SIR – It is time to ask the public if they would prefer Prince Andrew to Keir Starmer as Prime Minister.
 It would be close.

Bob Hart
Newark, Nottinghamshire

SIR – I offer "Starmite" as a cognomen for our leader. You either love him or you hate him.

Fred Crisp
Sheffield, South Yorkshire

The wurst of times

SIR – The Prime Minister has called for a ceasefire in Gaza and the return of the "sausages".
 Is he advocating the use of salami tactics?

Lawrence Littlestone
Edgware, Middlesex

SIR – Latest: Starmer declares war on Greggs.

Denis Tucker
Dinas Powys, Glamorgan

SIR – Release sausages, pork chops, lamb cutlets and most other meats. But please, please, detain all Spam fritters and throw away the key.

Andrew McGrath
Teddington, Middlesex

Maggie Maggie Maggie Out Out Out

SIR – "Starmer took down 'unsettling' portrait of Thatcher from No 10", reads your headline. Was he frit?

Tim Barnsley
Berwick-upon-Tweed, Northumberland

SIR – Maybe Keir Starmer would be less unsettled if he put up a picture of Liz Truss.

Julian Badenoch
Cowes, Isle of Wight

SIR – May I ask you please not to publish any more photographs of Sir Keir Starmer as I find them unsettling.

Derek Wellman
Lincoln

Power dressing

SIR – I have read with some dismay that Sir Keir is no longer accepting donations towards his wardrobe. This I feel is a grave error of judgment on his behalf. I for one am very happy to coordinate fundraising and forward money to No 10 in order to see that he does not appear in his underwear in public.

Nicholas Faulkner
Tilford, Surrey

SIR – Sir Keir accepted cash for glasses from Lord Alli. Can't he see it was a bit short-sighted to make a spectacle of himself in that way?

I get my glasses from a well-known discount store and they look and work just fine. Using them I could have made far better decisions for the country than Sir Keir has.

Dan Hartley
Solihull, West Midlands

SIR – As potential Lottery winners my wife and I would like to advise all Cabinet ministers that we will not be making any donation of wonga or bundles of clothing: our advice is to save and (don't laugh) buy what you can afford.

Howard Boothroyd
Kirkburton, West Yorkshire

SIR – Although we are not members of the Labour Party, I should be immensely grateful to the Prime Minister for an introduction to Lord Alli; my wife joins me in this sentiment.

Philip Black
Cheltenham, Gloucestershire

SIR – Rumours are abounding that the Prime Minister is in urgent need of a dozen pairs of new underpants and that a donor is being sought to facilitate the purchase of these. Could there be a peerage in it?

Trevor Burrage
Oxted, Surrey

SIR – I wouldn't mind politicians receiving a clothes allowance, provided that they could only spend it on a specially designed uniform, which they have to wear whenever they are working.

I suggest that it is made from sackcloth and ashes.

Matthew Darroch-Thompson
Bury St Edmunds, Suffolk

SIR – Why can't Keir Starmer use the same gentlemen's outfitter as Volodymyr Zelensky?

Derek Reed
Exmouth, Devon

SIR – It is glaringly obvious that Sir Keir Starmer is in desperate need of a backbone, but with the current state of NHS waiting lists, it seems unlikely he will get one during the course of this Government. For the sake of our nation I suggest we try to persuade Lord Alli to pay for him to receive one privately.

Philip Evans
Chippenham, Wiltshire

I'm afraid there is no money

SIR – Eating 12 grapes at midnight on New Year's Eve is a tradition that is said to bring good luck and prosperity in the coming year. I suggest that Starmer et al have a New Year's Eve party in the House of Commons wine cellar. Drinking 12 glasses each should solve the national debt crisis.

Susan Bischler
Malvern, Worcestershire

SIR – Once the vote on the assisted dying Bill
has passed, perhaps the Government can turn its
attention to the state of the economy which is going
the same way.

Roger Cousins
Beaconsfield, Buckinghamshire

SIR – It took the Labour government of James
Callaghan and Denis Healey six years to get to the
point where the IMF had to be called in to rescue the
economy. Keir Starmer and Rachel Reeves are almost
there in just six months. That's progress for you.

Michael Tyce
Oxford

SIR – Alongside the Fixed-term Parliaments Act, I
propose a Fixed-term Parliamentary Blame Act. Under
this legislation, an incoming administration would
only be able to blame the previous administration
for the state of the economy, the crisis in the NHS,
the ballooning immigration figures, or any other
governmental matter for a fixed period of time.

This would give the new government extra
motivation to solve such problems, and reduce the
time the public has to put up with the constant refrain
of "not our fault, blame the last lot".

Richard Allport
Hatfield, Hertfordshire

SIR – I've now heard the Labour Party talk about the disaster of the last 14 years so many times that I'm starting to think that they weren't all that bad.

> **Terence Flynn**
> Falmouth, Cornwall

SIR – David Lammy: "Britain is back". Back to the 1970s? Those of us of a certain age remember it well. Please, not again.

> **Alan Phizacklea**
> Marlborough, Wiltshire

Sir Keir's tunnel vision

SIR – The Prime Minister's claim that there is light at the end of the tunnel is to be welcomed. However if the light is to be delivered by clean British energy then it will be a long time coming and extremely expensive.

> **Dr Richard A. E. Grove**
> Isle of Whithorn, Wigtownshire

SIR – When my wife was bursar of a school in Sussex she had a sign in her office saying: "I thought I saw light at the end of the tunnel but it was some bugger with a torch bringing more work".

> **M. Burbidge**
> Bexhill-on-Sea, East Sussex

SIR – How long will it be before Starmer says "we are turning off the light at the end of the tunnel as an economy measure"?

Donald Massey
Great Haywood, Staffordshire

SIR – The Chancellor says "I can see the prize on offer if we make the right choices now". I visit a pub that has a sign outside saying "Free beer tomorrow". I don't believe the landlord either.

Lee Goodall
Churchdown, Gloucestershire

Growing pains

SIR – Whenever Rachel Reeves mentions "kickstarting growth", a wry smile comes over my face.

Anyone who rode motorcycles in the 1960s, when you had to kickstart them, will recall the excruciating pain when it kicked back. The engine would not start if you were clumsy setting the choke, throttle and ignition retard, forgot to tickle the carburettor and did not position the pistons just past top dead centre, before trying to kickstart it. 650cc of explosive mixture could then send the engine backwards 180 degrees and shoot the kickstarter back up in a long hammer blow through the sole of your foot.

It seems that the country, through the Chancellor's unwise positioning and clumsy actions, is about to experience its economic equivalent.

Simon Goddard
Twickenham, Middlesex

SIR – The only growth I can see is the growth in speeches about growth by this clueless Government.

Philip Dodd
Wooburn Moor, Buckinghamshire

Don't quit the day job

SIR – It would appear that Sir Keir Starmer's pronouncements have already had an effect on those considered economically inactive, given that Oasis are coming out of retirement and embarking on a world tour.

John Firrell
Litton Cheney, Dorset

SIR – The Prime Minister suggests that more people should work from home.

I will be interested to see how the tradesmen who are going to build all these new houses will manage this.

Maybe they could lay bricks using a drone.

Richard Matkin
Rolleston on Dove, Staffordshire

SIR – I spent more than 40 years working as an NHS dentist. I now feel that I missed out as I was never allowed to work from home.

Peter Rosie BDS
Ringwood, Hampshire

SIR – The chap who cuts my grass has just told me that in future he will be working from home. He tells me he will be thinking very hard about my lawn and the price will remain the same.

Gordon Davis
Cheltenham, Gloucestershire

SIR – In years past it would be traditional for readers to write to the editor and report hearing the first cuckoo of spring. However, I find a more reliable indicator of the advent of *tempus vernum* is the announcement by the National Education Union of their intention to call strike action. I can report that spring has arrived.

P. L. Pratt
Copthorne, West Sussex

SIR – When I grow up I want to be a sivil servant, not one of the hard ones like teecher or nurse or police ossifer, but one where I can do things in my bedroom wearing my pyjamas. When I am too old to work, they will make everyone call me Sir because I have been there so long and I also want them to give me a big penshin coz I think I will deserve it.

Iain Findley (age 63 and a half)
Audlem, Cheshire

But nobody's home

SIR – The Deputy Prime Minister will struggle to build one million houses in five years. Might I suggest that she should rather aim for the more attainable five houses in one million years.

N. Kessel
London N2

Labour in vain

SIR – This Labour Government is going to have to go some to be as bad as the last Tory one, but in fairness, they've made a jolly good start.

David Watt
Lasham, Hampshire

SIR – I am rapidly coming to the conclusion that "The Labour Party" is one of the more unfortunate misnomers of the present century.

Paul Trim
McGregor, Western Cape, South Africa

SIR – Now that the Labour Party is more interested in pursuing "woke" policies, rather than looking after the interests of ordinary working people, isn't it about time to change the name to something more appropriate? My own suggestion is the Dinner Party.

Roger Kemp
London N8

SIR – A rumour has reached us here in New Zealand. We understand the four Great Officers of State are all soon to be reassigned to duties more reflective of their experience and abilities.

According to this rumour, the Chancellor is to become a kindergarten teacher, the Home Secretary is about to train as a window washer, and the Foreign Secretary will shortly open a whelk stall in Blackpool for the summer season.

As for the Prime Minister, if this rumour is correct we shall see him appearing as a contestant on *Britain's Got Talent*, singing that great song, "It's My Party (And I'll Cry If I Want To)".

Can your sources please confirm or deny this for us?

Graham Sharpe
Wellington, New Zealand

Reeves on the line

SIR – The Prime Minister has assured us that the Chancellor of the Exchequer will still be in place at the next election. With such a fervent endorsement, Rachel Reeves should start wrapping her glasses and china.

Mike Tickner
Winterbourne Earls, Wiltshire

SIR – Your headline "Reeves takes axe to Civil Service" is, I feel, a touch optimistic. Given that she is a Labour Chancellor of the Exchequer I would suggest that nail scissors would be more the order of the day.

Neil Abrey
Petersfield, Hampshire

SIR – In making her recent changes to welfare payments and meeting the aspirations of the less well off, Rachel Reeves would have done well to have looked to Charles Dickens.

He knew that there are no great expectations without Pip.

Chris Harris
New Malden, Surrey

SIR – Currently my *bêtes noires* are moles and lawn-digging badgers.

By the time we reach October, I am expecting that they will have been superseded by Rachel Reeves (and her Budget).

Shaun Allison
Bramshill, Hampshire

SIR – I am sure readers will have plenty of suggestions for Rachel Reeves of replacement artwork for display at No 11.

I would like to nominate Edvard Munch's *Despair* (if the current owner was happy to oblige).

Joanne Stanley-Jones
Waterlooville, Hampshire

SIR – Your front-page picture of Rachel Reeves in tears is exactly how I felt after her disastrous Budget was announced earlier this year.

P. S. Badger
Worcester

SIR – Keir Starmer has achieved what I previously thought impossible – he has made the nation feel sorry for Rachel Reeves.

Jolyon Grey
Cheltenham, Gloucestershire

SIR – No one knows how long the Chancellor of the Exchequer will remain in her post.

However, we can be assured that it will at least seem a very, very long time.

Tim Instone
Bath, Somerset

The richer, the poorer

SIR – According to Sir Keir Starmer, "Those with the broadest shoulders should bear the heavier burden."

It seems all those seniors' gym memberships are finally going to pay off.

Dr Alf Crossman
Rudgwick, West Sussex

SIR – I suggest, for Keir Starmer's anthem, the Beatles song "Taxman".

It includes the lines:
If you try to sit, I'll tax your seat
If you get too cold, I'll tax the heat
If you take a walk, I'll tax your feet
Now my advice for those who die
Declare the pennies on your eyes.

Tony Cummings
Henley-on-Thames, Oxfordshire

SIR – I am amazed that our beady-eyed Chancellor has, so far, overlooked a national source of income.

Children, your pocket money is at risk.

Noel Sudbury
Topsham, Devon

SIR – Sir Keir Starmer promised me my council tax wouldn't go up by a single penny. Well, he's a man of his word; it hasn't gone up a single penny. It's gone up by £300.

Joseph Kennils
Little Wigborough, Essex

SIR – I can't help feeling this Government will stick to its promise of not punching us in the face in order to justify kicking us in the teeth instead.

Phil Angell
Helston, Cornwall

SIR – Having just bought a new television I thought it advisable not to watch the spending review, thus sparing it from possibly irreparable damage.

Having read *The Daily Telegraph* this morning, I know I made the right choice.

Andy Vale
Upminster, Essex

SIR – To quote Noel Coward: "Hurray, hurray, hurray, Misery's here to stay". But will there be good times around the corner?

Stuart Geddes
Tregagle, Monmouthshire

SIR – I wonder what kind of grovelling apology we now owe to Liz Truss.

Philip Franklin
Wellesbourne, Warwickshire

Work farce

SIR – Further to Sir Keir Starmer's pledge not to increase taxes on working people, I recently saw a Mercedes Benz AMG with the number plate YIWORK.

Mal Locke
Queensland, Australia

SIR – Cabinet ministers have suggested that anyone who earns more than £100,000 a year is not considered a "working person". As the Prime Minister and all Cabinet ministers earn more than £100,000, by this definition they are not working people. If they are not working then it is no surprise that the Government is in such a mess.

Robert F. Ashton
Shrewsbury, Shropshire

SIR – Given the Prime Minister's difficulty with defining a working person, perhaps we should pray that no-one asks him to define a working woman.

John Sadler
Berriew, Montgomeryshire

Mutterings from Ambridge

SIR – With the inheritance tax on farms, does this mean the end of *The Archers*?

Jacky Offen
Maidstone, Kent

SIR – Instead of taxing good farmers who make good decisions, why not tax bad politicians who make bad decisions? There are plenty of them.

Richard Cavendish
Ashburton, Devon

SIR – Perhaps if all our farmers produced avocados they might be treated more sympathetically.

Ivor Gibson
Loughton, Essex

SIR – I get it now. If the Government can goad our farmers into going on strike, the resulting food shortages would help solve the obesity crisis. Sheer genius.

Jane Moth
Stone, Staffordshire

So long, farewell

SIR – Will the last non-dom to leave the country please switch the lights off – assuming that Ed Miliband has not already done so.

> **Paul Fairweather**
> Henley-on-Thames, Oxfordshire

SIR – With a new twist it seems that under Starmer socialism we are running out of other people.

> **Keith Macpherson**
> Clevedon, Somerset

SIR – Yvette Cooper has a plan. Rachel Reeves has a plan. Angela Rayner has a plan. What's the collective noun for a group of Baldricks?

> **Jeni Kenyon**
> Bristol

SIR – Of the seven deadly sins I reckon the Labour Party has already demonstrated five of the seven: pride, greed, lust, envy and wrath.

C'mon gluttony and sloth!

> **Peter Forrest**
> London N6

SIR – I hope that all of those who wrote letters before the election saying that they would never vote Tory again and were transferring their allegiance to Reform UK, the Lib Dems or the Monster Raving Loony Party are satisfied with the result of their efforts. For myself, I am happy to be able to identify with the car stickers I remember from the Harold Wilson era: "Don't blame me, I voted Conservative".

Richard Piper
Ickenham, Middlesex

The cold shoulder

SIR – Not all of the prisoners being released early will be celebrating and praising Keir Starmer.

Please spare a thought for those of pensionable age, who will be climbing the walls to get back inside where the heating's on.

John Knowles
Berkhamsted, Hertfordshire

SIR – A few years ago a pensioner friend was still playing cricket in the team which I captained. He had used his winter fuel payment to buy a cricket bat, claiming that if the worst situation arose he could burn the bat in the hearth.

Neil Lambert
Halifax, West Yorkshire

SIR – I think we should start a movement called Old Lives Matter.

I would not recommend taking the knee however, as we wouldn't be able to get up again.

Kathleen Glennon
Newcastle upon Tyne

SIR – As a pensioner, is there a union I can join?

Jane Beazer
Bristol

SIR – Would it help if I returned the 25p a week extra pension I gleefully received on turning 80?

I can't post it back as it will take six weeks to save up for a stamp.

Diana Berridge
Blandford Forum, Dorset

SIR – I do hope that one of the 243 questions for pensioners applying for pension credit asks whether the applicant is pregnant.

Graeme Williams
West Malling, Kent

SIR – With additional winter fuel payments to be set out in the November Budget and so unlikely to be paid before Christmas, it seems Sir Keir Starmer cannot even make a convincing U-turn; it is more of a J-walk.

Edward Hill
Chandlers Ford, Hampshire

SIR – It seems to me that the Government's policies are rather similar to the perception of the weather in Scotland, where they say that if you don't like the current weather then just wait five minutes and it will change.

John Marsh
Sheringham, Norfolk

SIR – The Chancellor is going to means-test eligibility for the winter fuel allowance. My wife tells me that I am very good at being mean, so I move forward with confidence and expectation, even though my income is over the required limit.

Scott Clapworthy
Shrewsbury, Shropshire

Signs of intelligent life

SIR – Has anyone considered developing an AI Prime Minister? I suspect it might be an interesting proposition, given the present incumbent. Might we not notice a difference?

Rosy Drohan
Marksbury, Somerset

SIR – Sir Keir Starmer believes his plans to turbocharge Artificial Intelligence will increase growth and boost living standards. If you key "Artificial Intelligence" into a thesaurus it rereads as "Fake Ability".

Angus Long
Newcastle upon Tyne

SIR – What this Government lacks is not Artificial Intelligence but Actual Intelligence.

Mary Moore
Croydon, Surrey

Missing in action

SIR – When our children were small the regular chorus of demands, disagreements, opinions and accusations could sometimes be wearing but was at least to be expected. We very quickly learnt, however, to be more concerned by prolonged silences. These usually meant that mischief was being plotted or brought to fruition.

For one never normally shy of the headlines, Angela Rayner has been suspiciously quiet for a while now.

Charles Smith-Jones
Landrake, Cornwall

SIR – Whatever happened to Sue Gray? Should we send out a search party?

Mike Bingham
Alvechurch, Worcestershire

SIR – I am thinking of sending Sir Keir a greetings card. Can anyone advise which continent I should mail it to?

Mike Donaldson
Southampton

SIR – Seeking missing UK Prime Minister – last seen in the US, Germany, France, Ireland, Italy, Belgium, Samoa, Hungary, Azerbaijan, Brazil, the United Arab Emirates and Saudi Arabia.

Upcoming trips for possible future sightings: Saudi Arabia, Cyprus, Canada, the Netherlands, South Africa.

If found, please ask (and you'll have to be quick) whether the taxpayer is paying for all these trips, and what will happen to all those air miles.

P.J. Mills
Dursley, Gloucestershire

On the rubbish heap

SIR – I am alarmed to hear about the bin trouble in Birmingham. I have suggested to my family there that perhaps if they were to sing the Bin Song to the men involved, their area might be exempted. "No two people have ever bin so in love, bin so in love, bin so in love, etc, etc."

You never know, it might soften their hearts.

Guy Rose
London SW14

SIR – It is a pity that HS2 is not available at the moment, as it would afford quick travel to Londoners wishing to look at the Birmingham rats. By the time the railway is finished they will probably have grown from cat size to Shetland pony size.

Michael Holman
St Lawrence, Jersey

Where there's smoke

SIR – I gave up smoking on June 21, 2001 and have not had a cigarette since. However, Keir Starmer's plan to ban smoking in pub gardens and public spaces may just be enough to persuade me to take it up again.

Archie Graham-Palmer
Wrexham, Denbighshire

SIR – The logical next step for the Prime Minister to reduce the burden on the NHS further is to ban alcohol, sweets, sticky toffee pudding and quite possibly leaving the confines of one's home.

Roger Wilson
Charter Alley, Hampshire

SIR – I have no problem with a person's right to smoke: just put them together in an enclosed area, as we do with kippers.

Barrie Taylor
Highcliffe, Dorset

SIR – If this Government does much more to discourage the use of pubs, even more people will meet and chat to their neighbours while blocking the aisles of the local supermarket.

Howard Stephens
Burgh St Peter, Norfolk

Battle of the sexes

SIR – The scholars who have identified 93 depictions of male genitalia on the Bayeux Tapestry are to be congratulated on the diligence of their research. Perhaps they should now turn their attention to investigating the transgender nature of the soldiers, who appear to be wearing skirts.

Peter Harper
Lover, Wiltshire

SIR – The Science Museum argues that Lego promotes heterosexuality.

I would disagree: the Lego brick is clearly trans-gender as it is male on the top and female on the bottom.

Keith Jones
Broad Hinton, Wiltshire

SIR – Now the courts have helped our witless politicians clarify what a man and a woman are, perhaps they could also clarify whether Liberal Democrats can identify as Tories.

Paul Gaynor
Windermere, Cumbria

SIR – The Prime Minister required the Supreme Court to provide clarity in defining a woman. I am an old queen and I have known what one is since puberty descended and my mind drifted away from Barbie dolls to Ken.

Mark Peaker
London W1

SIR – Phew! Glad Keir Starmer has understood the difficult concept of "a woman". He must have been "away when we did that" for the biology lessons, unless, like my school, it was discussed with reference to rabbits and he didn't make the connection. If so, he is probably still wondering how he missed the stork or forgot about the gooseberry bush at the bottom of the garden.

Jeannette Meyers
Ashford, Kent

SIR – Several years ago we enjoyed a fantastic holiday in New Zealand.

One evening after having a meal in a local pub and while paying a visit to their facilities I was intrigued to find their solution to the gender debate.

On offer was a choice of three doors, each with a different sign:
- Cows
- Bulls
- The rest of the herd.

J. Anderson
Crieff, Perthshire

SIR – Our six-year-old granddaughter, who lives in London, came to stay with us on her own over the Easter break. She is completely obsessed with our eight-year-old dog and one morning announced that she wished she was "a boy dog", spending the morning with the dog in his basket.

I am now concerned that the police may not be properly prepared for any trans canine protests that may take place in London, organised by our granddaughter, and hope that they will ensure the safety of monuments such as the Animals in War statue in Park Lane should any vandalism, involving Bonios, take place.

For my part, I am a huge J.K. Howling fan and hope that she will continue to demand protected spaces for dogs (and especially bitches) both in kennels and vets' waiting rooms.

Alison Varney
Abingdon, Oxfordshire

SIR – In the light of the recent furore surrounding a "gender-fluid" dachshund, I would like it known that I remain 100 per cent canine-male and not any other neutral variation. I will continue to respond positively to "good boy" or "good dog", but not "good girl" or "good it" as my owners have struggled to get me even this far in training.

Yours obediently (sometimes),

Jeff the three-year-old Jack Russell
(Fred and Jane Pennell
Bournemouth, Dorset)

Some local damage

SIR – On my way out for a lunchtime pint I went to
the dog poo bin and the polling station. In my dotage
I hope that I dropped things off in the right order.

Dave Alsop
Gloucester

SIR – Sir Keir Starmer promised change.
This probably isn't the sort he intended!

Alan Hetherington
Stillington, North Yorkshire

SIR – Looks like we're heading for a Reform-nation.

John Anthony
London E11

SIR – Should Kemi Badenoch and Nigel Farage
decide to combine forces I suggest it be known as the
ReformaTory Party.

Carolyn Andrews
Bournemouth, Dorset

SIR – I hear it is rumoured the Reform Party is in
the process of changing its name to the Hokey Cokey
Party.

Barrie Taylor
Christchurch, Dorset

The youth will out

SIR – The Government proposes a reduction in the voting age to 16.

Will it now be able to claim that the children are back in the room?

Jon Brokenshire
Sevenoaks, Kent

SIR – You can promise a 16-year-old anything and they will believe you and want to support you. Unless of course you are the parent, in which case they will not believe you and want to support anybody but you.

Dr Richard Hiles
Thirsk, North Yorkshire

SIR – In my 35 years as a teacher I regularly held debates in the classroom and as part of extra-curricular activities.

It was noticeable that the voting would frequently be swung by the most charismatic speaker.

Does Keir Starmer really fancy his chances?

Linda Beskeen
Redruth, Cornwall

Now that the party's over

SIR – Scientists at Colossal Biosciences in the US are attempting to bring back extinct species. I wonder if they could be persuaded to resurrect an earlier and more successful version of the Conservative Party.

Martin Bastone
East Grinstead, West Sussex

SIR – Should Conservative MPs decide to form a football team, Kemi Badenoch would most certainly be excluded. There is little point in selecting someone who, as evidenced at PMQs, spectacularly misses every opportunity when presented with an open goal.

Graham W. Swift
Newcastle-under-Lyme, Staffordshire

SIR – Robert Tombs has written a piece entitled "History shows Kemi is the right choice for Conservative leader". He may well be quite correct; but a search on Badenoch and history brings up the 14th-century Wolf of Badenoch, a Scottish prince who burnt down Elgin Cathedral and was subsequently excommunicated. Still, it is over 400 years since Guy Fawkes tried something similar at Westminster, so it's probably high time that Parliament was relocated.

Tom Stubbs
Surbiton, Surrey

SIR – I wonder if it is the ambition of the Conservative Party to change its leader more often than Manchester United FC replaces its manager.

John Catchpole
Beverley, East Yorkshire

SIR – James Cleverly's constituency is Braintree. Someone's bright idea?

Fiona Wild
Cheltenham, Gloucestershire

SIR – Mr Cleverly struggles to live up to his name. I sympathise.

David Money
Cambridge

Left to their own devices

SIR – If Zara Sultana and Jeremy Corbyn are stuck for a name for their new party, might I suggest the Fruit and Nut Party?

Graham Wilson
Deeping St James, Cambridgeshire

SIR – It is a pity that the Monster Raving Loony Party is already taken.

Tim Hadland
Northampton

SIR – "Oooh, Jeremy Corbyn".
Well, that's the Glastonbury chants for next summer sorted.

Peter Hopper
Newmarket, Suffolk

The art of the deal

SIR – Starmer going to negotiate with the EU is rather like the hapless apprentice told to go and buy a tin of striped paint.

Keith Chambers
Brockenhurst, Hampshire

SIR – It is now glaringly obvious that the only thing that our Prime Minister is able to negotiate successfully is a staircase.
Everything else is simply beyond him.

Peter Gilbert
Ross-on-Wye, Herefordshire

SIR – It's an F all round for Labour. First Sir Keir went after the farmers, now it's the fishermen. Watch out if you're a fireman or, dare I say it, a Freemason.

Robert Tuck
West Runton, Norfolk

SIR – For sale – one fishing fleet (no longer required), complete with crossed red lines, broken manifesto promises, discarded principles and moral flexibility. Apply to 10 Downing St, London, SW1A 2AA.

Max Sawyer
Stamford, Lincolnshire

SIR – It's nowt but kipperulation.

Alan Orton
Leamington Spa, Warwickshire

SIR – We should send a small group of car-traders to deal with the EU. They'd recognise our strengths and the results would be very different.

John Lavender
Port Erin, Isle of Man

SIR – Yes, there were many betrayals by our PM in the misnamed EU "reset negotiations", but look on the bright side – it could have been the Lib Dems doing the negotiating, in which case we would be forced to eat croissants every morning, drink Euro-fizz in the pub and be required to drive on the right hand side of the road, in return for the EU having to watch *Coronation Street* and *EastEnders*.

Alan Brown
Medstead, Hampshire

SIR – I am all for rejoining the EU, but only if we can replace France.

> **Anthony Stansfeld**
> Kintbury, Berkshire

From zero to nothing

SIR – Sorting out our bookshelves yesterday I came across our *Where's Wally* book and it made me think of Ed Miliband, our Energy and Climate Change Secretary.

Has anyone seen him?

> **Alexandra Elletson**
> Marlborough, Wiltshire

SIR – Rachel Reeves's (third Heathrow runway) and Ed Miliband's (net zero emissions at all costs) conflicting policies make me wonder if the Left hand knows what the further Left hand is doing.

> **Rodney Chadburn**
> Ipswich, Suffolk

SIR – "Putin ready to cripple Britain in cyber war", reads your headline.

Why bother? Ed Miliband and his energy policies will achieve it without any effort from Russia.

> **Lindsay Pearson**
> Ashfield, Suffolk

SIR – Is it time for an official petition for a new title for the Secretary of State, more in keeping with the reality of the job?

Perhaps something like "Secretary of State for Renewable Energy, at any cost and now, and with zero chance of simultaneous electricity for all".

Michael Pritchard
Hemel Hempstead, Hertfordshire

SIR – Someone needs to tell Ed Miliband that if you're going to commit an act of self-harm – don't be a world leader in it.

John Clezy
Adderbury, Oxfordshire

SIR – My grandmother once told me that any man who cannot eat a bacon sandwich gracefully should not be entrusted with running our power infrastructure.

Bob Caunter
Teignmouth, Devon

SIR – Ed Miliband is planning to attend the next COP summit, which is being held in Brazil.

Perhaps we can slow down his mad race to net zero by sending him there by dinghy.

The weeks spent at sea give us time to mitigate some of his policies, at the same time reducing his carbon footprint.

Christopher H Jones
Glasgow

SIR – My wife has just built a beautiful one-twelfth scale model of a Georgian kitchen. It occurs to me that if all terrier owners volunteered their dogs to run round in an old-fashioned spit-wheel as was the case in those days, we might be able to help with Ed Miliband's inevitable power blackouts.

Whether today's terriers would agree is of course quite another matter.

Charles Barrington
Great Bealings, Suffolk

SIR – I feel the latest report from the Climate Change Committee urging us to cut our meat and dairy consumption by half may well backfire. The extra noxious gas produced by 60 million or so flatulent humans on a plant-based diet may well negate any savings from avoiding meat and dairy products.

Brian Hodgetts
Honiton, Devon

SIR – Net zero would be a more attractive proposal if it included an immediate ban on the use of petrol-powered leaf blowers.

Roger Jackson
Stockport, Cheshire

Bricks and Stones

SIR – As your report reminds us, Sir Michael Jagger has often vocally bemoaned the fact that he has been unable to get no satisfaction; and his victory in successfully objecting to the construction of a 29-storey tower confirms his continuing inability to obtain no satisfaction.

I feel sure that this will not be the last time we will see Jagger's determination to not fade away in the face of adversity. He has certainly shown developers that you can't always get what you want.

At least Jagger can take comfort that it's all over now (until someone else makes him angry).

Nicholas Young
London W13

SIR – May we borrow Mick Jagger to save our green belt?

Tricia Barnes
Beaconsfield, Buckinghamshire

Matters of life and death

SIR – The Bill to legalise assisted dying is an emotive and polarising subject, and I too have concerns about all the safeguarding issues it raises.

However, if Diane Abbott is passionately opposed to the Bill, perhaps Parliament has got it right after all.

David Vincent
Cranbrook, Kent

SIR – At a recent visit to Harrogate hospital I noticed there was a "discharge lounge" where patients are given medication and appropriate advice before leaving the hospital following treatment.

If the parliamentary Bill currently with the House of Lords is to become law the hospital will probably require a "dispatch lounge".

It is to be hoped each is clearly labelled.

Michael Stephenson
Leeds, West Yorkshire

Repeat proscription

SIR – It seems to me the only purpose of the Senedd in Cardiff is to invoke bans on things from which normal people derive enjoyment. Greyhound racing is apparently next on the list. At the current rate there will soon be nothing left to ban in Wales except perhaps not being Welsh.

Ian Mackenzie
Preston, Lancashire

SIR – I wondered whether I was dreaming when I read that the Scottish National Party may be introducing a ban on domestic cats. If this really happens, there will be an influx of cat-owning Scots to England. Presumably, if only English wildlife is decimated by Scottish cats, this would be most agreeable to the SNP, despite the loss of potential voters.

Fiona Wild
Cheltenham, Gloucestershire

Take to the streets

SIR – As this Government is keen to improve productivity, perhaps ministers should contact the organisation and funding source of the *Socialist Worker,* as clearly they are able to produce an immediate, endless supply of placards for whichever group wishes to cause a demonstration in London at the weekend.

David Johnstone
Pewsey, Wiltshire

Welcome to Britain

SIR – I have been gathering information from various articles published in your newspaper and have come to the conclusion that I have discovered the masterplan of Sir Keir Starmer and Yvette Cooper to stem the tide of illegal immigrants.

They intend to make the United Kingdom such a miserable place to live that people will just stop coming.

B. W. Perkes
Sutton Coldfield, West Midlands

SIR – This morning I switched on the radio only to hear Keir Starmer talking about Labour's latest policy on immigration. After five minutes of waffle and wind I could take no more and switched off. He hadn't even started to describe the policy itself.

It dawns on me that here is the solution to the immigration problem: subject anyone arriving illegally to endless Starmer speeches. They would soon be pleading to leave.

Tom Williams
Sheffield, South Yorkshire

SIR – Now a dog has crossed the English Channel in a small boat of illegal migrants, and has been put into quarantine for at least four months, at some cost to the taxpayer. When the dog is eventually released into the community, I suggest that it be rehomed in Barking.

Martin Coomber
London SW19

SIR – At last our Home Secretary has found the solution to illegal Channel crossings. She is going to pray for bad weather. I wish I'd thought of that.

David Steer
Wellington, Somerset

SIR – Your report that the Government is to adopt a "one in, one out" migration policy.

Any chance that the first one out could be Sir Keir Starmer?

Mark Hudson
Ashford, Kent

Me, myself and ID

SIR – I have an ID card which should have been renewed in 1962. A bit too late to do it now I suppose.

William Boog-Scott
Chalfont St Peter, Buckinghamshire

SIR – When most skiing resorts started to demand photo identity on the ski pass, I was behind a person (difficult to determine gender in full ski outfit) whose photo on their pass was of a mountain gorilla.

They passed the security with no problem.

Patrick White
London SW20

SIR – In the non-digital age of the 1980s I used to gain access to Test matches at Lord's by flashing a packet of Marlboro Red cigarettes to the turnstile attendant. This only worked when following close behind and chatting to a friend who had shown his red MCC pass book to the turnstile attendant just before me. Nine times out of ten the attendant assumed my red pack of cigarettes was also a pass book and allowed me entry to the ground.

Murray Tollemache
Bentworth, Hampshire

Cheese it, the cops!

SIR – Twenty-four tons of fancy cheese has been stolen from a British dairy company. It might be worth checking to see if that included Wensleydale cheese. If it did then add Wallace and Gromit to the suspect list.

Dennis Fitzgerald
Melbourne, Australia

SIR – I was interested to read about the growth of cannabis in the former Wildings department store in Newport.

Of all the potential uses for our monolith here in Guildford I had not thought of a Greenhouse of Fraser, but it could catch on.

Peter Robinson
Guildford, Surrey

SIR – I was amused by the news that a convicted shoplifter, as punishment, must now use a see-through bag when she goes shopping. Probably inadequate. Surely the only reliable deterrent would be see-through clothing as well.

Martyn Redmore
Huntingdon

SIR – Home Secretary Yvette Cooper is considering requiring knives to have rounded tips. I assume this will become known as a Cooper knife as it would not be the sharpest one in the drawer.

Nigel Algar
Bottesford, Nottinghamshire

SIR – It's pertinent that in China, in 2017, a man killed three women with a single chopstick.

Clearly, the moral of the tale is to make it law that food preparation is banned: only processed foods to be eaten, with a straw.

Douglas Clerk
Stanley, Perthshire

I predict a riot

SIR – The third round of each *Great British Bake Off* episode should now be renamed the "Riotstopper Challenge", with the task being to bake a Two-Tier Policing Cake.

Bob Lyddon
Wells-next-the-Sea, Norfolk

SIR – I think looting your local Greggs is flawed as a critique of multiculturalism.

Phil Saunders
Bungay, Suffolk

SIR – The Government may have been a little hasty in cancelling the Rwanda arrangements out of hand. There may now be considerable support for keeping the migrants here, and sending our home-grown thugs to Rwanda in their place.

Dan Lyon
Lytham St Annes, Lancashire

SIR – In the 19th century the solution to prison over-crowding was either hanging or transportation to Australia. Rwanda is closer and they play cricket there too.

William Fleming
Frimley, Surrey

Every creed and colour

SIR – The racist graffiti "NO WHITES" in Birmingham took me back to the early 1960s in Kilburn, northwest London, where "NO BLACKS" was once scrawled on a wall. Before any action could be taken, a different hand had added: "Or Whites" under the first message. Two days later, a third hand wrote: "That's OK, I'm Brown." I suggest that residents of Birmingham, where there is no shortage of first-class comedians, could similarly turn anger into humour by coming up with their own additions.

Garry May
Haddenham, Buckinghamshire

The hating game

SIR – The massed chorus chanting of "the referee's a w—-r" at hundreds of professional league football matches each weekend, involving hundreds of thousands of fans, clearly qualifies as a non-crime hate incident and the police should investigate accordingly.

Roger Wilson
Charter Alley, Hampshire

SIR – I am concerned that the local rozzers might call at my house later in the day and drag me off for a spot of the third degree.

This is because I have committed so many non-crimes since I woke this morning, including getting up (hateful to the bedridden), having a shower (loathed by aquaphobes), getting dressed (insulting to nudists) and having a cup of coffee (anathema to tea-drinkers).

Edward Windham-Bellord
Cucklington, Somerset

SIR – I shall in future keep my weekly copy of *The Spectator* under the carpet. Keeping it in my underwear drawer would be tempting fate.

Nigel Beale
Poole, Dorset

SIR – To plagiarise René Descartes: "I think, therefore I'm likely to be arrested".

Alisdair Keats-Rawling
Stockport, Cheshire

Pure imagination

SIR – The Government plans to give children young as five the critical thinking skills to identify misinformation and fake news. Have they considered the impact on Santa Claus and the Tooth Fairy?

Ronnie Bradford
Vienna, Austria

SIR – Though Michael Deacon points out that saying "fairies aren't real" may upset a child, my childhood experience was distinctly different.

Thanks to bedtime reading, I learnt that every time I said "I don't believe in fairies", one of their number would expire. Of course, I now appreciate that my supposed achievements aren't particularly susceptible to scientific validation, which is arguably good enough reason to desist from the practice.

Richard Weeks
Felixstowe, Suffolk

Here endeth the lesson

SIR – The discussion continues to rage as to whether a one-word summary is appropriate when assessing schools.

I am reminded that in Genesis when God created the world that at the end of each day He came to the conclusion that it was "good".

One word worked for Him.

Mark Wade
Reading, Berkshire

SIR – My name is M. Poppins, your Ofsted inspector. There will soon be changes to our reports – however here is my verdict for today.

Supercalifragilisticexpialidocious.

Bernard Powell
Southport, Lancashire

Sitting on defence

SIR – Having delivered an ambulance to a unit on the
eastern front in Ukraine and returned to the UK by
military vehicle, minibus, train and plane, I have just
been told by Great Western staff that I am not allowed
to carry a coffee along the train as it is too dangerous.

Oddly that wasn't considered a problem on the
train leaving Kramatorsk with the sound of Russian
artillery and air raid sirens accompanying the
departure.

I am not overly convinced we are particularly ready
mentally to go to war.

Adrian Simpson
Thurlestone, Devon

SIR – We currently have just under 20,000 Regular
Army Infantry soldiers – but I take comfort from the
fact that we have 32,000 police officers in London.
Perhaps it would be simpler to arrest the Russian army.

Richard Beattie
Tisbury, Wiltshire

SIR – As a junior officer trying to figure out the
difference between soft and hard power, I was advised
that soft power is the "Beware of the Dog" sign on the
garden gate and hard power is the 100lb Rottweiler
standing behind it.

Lt Col Lyndon Robinson (retd)
Mursley, Buckinghamshire

SIR – So how will the next conversation go between Our Great Leader and Putin?

"Look, Vlad, old chum, give us 10 years to get ready and then we've got what we call a game of cricket; all fair; all square…"

I'd rather dust off my Russian books.

Peter Kernick
Teddington, Middlesex

SIR – A new Home Guard will be formed to protect national infrastructure. I am far too old for the regular Forces but I will gladly volunteer for the new Guard. I am sure I will be excellent at channelling my inner Corporal.

Trevor Jones
Sidmouth, Devon

Halt – who goes there?

SIR – On holiday last week in the Cotswolds, I was only about ten miles from Brize Norton. Had I known the MoD was having trouble securing the base against pro-Palestinian activists, I could have loaned them the baby monitor we bought to check on my young granddaughter in our holiday home.

It had sound and video monitoring and you could speak to the baby – "Stop playing with that red paint". All for only £35 from Argos. Other retail outlets are available.

Geoff Longmire
Via email

SIR – Am I alone in thinking that, judging by Tim Sigsworth's report of the existing security measures outside RAF Brize Norton ("RAF base's only defence against Palestine Action was 6ft wooden fence"), the secret weapon in the defence of the UK appears to be No Mow May?

Rachel Penfound
Kettering, Northamptonshire

SIR – In the 1960s RAF Waddington in Lincolnshire housed three squadrons of Vulcan bombers, then charged with the nation's nuclear deterrent. The airfield was easily accessible from surrounding farmland, but the widely dispersed aircraft were patrolled by RAF police with vicious-looking attack dogs. As a junior officer, I once heard a charge against an airman who, on being asked for his identity card by a policeman, had slowly removed it from his pocket and then shown it to the dog.

Richard Fletcher RAF (retd)
Newmarket, Suffolk

Stop the world, I want to get off

SIR – In an article in Saturday's *Telegraph* Isabel Oakeshott says the country has "gone to the dogs". Sadly we can't even do that since most of the greyhound tracks have closed.

John Chillington
Wells, Somerset

SIR – I am incandescent with rage at this Government and absolutely everything they do, which leaves nothing in particular for me to write to you about.

Graham Underwood
Northampton

SIR – I wish to complain in the strongest possible terms about Sir Keir Starmer, Donald Trump, Vladimir Putin, the EU, China and people who sniff.

When I rule the world they will be the first up against the wall.

David Nunn
West Malling, Kent

SIR – When you become tired of news I suppose it could be said you are also tired of life. I'm getting there.

Camilla Coats-Carr
Teddington, Middlesex

HOME
THOUGHTS ON
ABROAD

No sex, please

SIR – In light of the draconian rules that the Taliban has imposed on women in Afghanistan, I wonder why they don't simply ban any contact whatsoever between men and women. The problem will be solved in one generation.

Mike Withers
Lytham St. Annes, Lancashire

An old enmity

SIR – Some might be curious why Iran holds the UK in such contempt.

The answer lies in the Hillman Hunter, a shabby and much maligned saloon car sold in the 1960s and 1970s in the UK but strangely still foisted on the unsuspecting motorists of Iran until well into the 2000s. No wonder they hate us.

Frank Hall
Ramsgate, Kent

Make America Great. Again.

SIR – Film 4's 9pm movie on the day of the US election was *Groundhog Day* – and that wasn't a last-minute switch.

Apparently the schedulers knew something about the outcome that the polling companies did not.

Next time I'll bet on whoever Channel 4 fancies.

Mike Wells
Ickwell, Bedfordshire

SIR – I'm a member of a small bridge club in east London. We are people of a certain age and follow our own rules. Part of the weekly event is a chat about politics. We are alarmed at what the new (old) president of the United States is doing in his dotage and have decided to make a stand. We have therefore adjusted our bidding process and only play no-Trump. We hope that this will have the desired effect.

John Anthony
London E11

SIR – If ever justification for a monarchy were needed, just look across the pond.

Jane Gelder
London SE1

SIR – Donald Trump? Never heard of him.
  Yours in control,

E.R. Musk
Mars 1
Via email

SIR – The anxieties provoked by the return of Donald Trump as the 47th president are exemplified by much of the correspondence today. I am reliably informed that as the Earth rotates on its axis around the Sun and we mere mortals experience dawn and dusk, there is no US executive order planned to rename these two Don and Musk.

Dr S. K. Goolamali
Northwood, Middlesex

SIR – Personally I am looking forward to Elon Musk launching the MMGA (Make Mars Great Again) mission from somewhere in the Gulf of America. I have a list of ideal candidates for the crew.

Dermot Flaherty
Southampton

SIR – If Elon Musk is still looking to cut wastage, he need look no further than abolishing Congress and the Senate, two quite expensive organisations the services of which the current administration clearly has no need whatsoever.

David Argent
Crondall, Hampshire

Trump on manoeuvres

SIR – In 1989 US president George H. W. Bush took over Panama in Operation Just Cause. News reports suggest that Donald Trump wants to take the Panama Canal and Greenland. This should be called Operation Just Because.

Geoff Moore
Alness, Ross-shire

SIR – Presumably President Trump's motive for incorporating Canada as the 51st State is that he will inherit an ice hockey team capable of beating Putin's.

Rod Mccarron
Porthleven, Cornwall

SIR – Donald Trump should save his money and forget buying Greenland.

Instead buy a down-at-heel little patch of real estate that needs knocking into shape and is a bit further south. Moreover it's going at a bargain basement price. Britain.

Angela Lawrence
Woodbridge, Suffolk

SIR – Father Christmas actually lives in Greenland. There may be some risk of Donald Trump being categorised as a naughty boy.

Mark Rand
Settle, North Yorkshire

SIR – In considering Mr Trump's interest in joining the Commonwealth, should we not be selective? Anywhere called an Empire State (New York) is clearly suitable, as is one with the Union Jack in their state flag (Hawaii), plus those named after British monarchs (Virginia, Carolinas, Georgia). However those with French names (Maine, Louisiana) must be doubtful: so too those with a rebellious history (Massachusetts).

Chris Jolly
Chigwell, Essex

SIR – Donald Trump might succeed in making America great, but not that great.

Peter Le Coyte
Dulverton, Somerset

Braggart-in-chief

SIR – I went down to my farm a few days ago and a cock pheasant in superb breeding condition was standing on a mound of earth with his chest all puffed out.

I could imagine him saying: "Look at me I'm great, look at me I really am great."

He reminded me of President Trump.

> **Nicholas Watts**
> Spalding, Lincolnshire

SIR – This weekend the annual Clown Convention took place in Bristol.

Was President Trump invited?

> **Ian Duckworth**
> Billington, Lancashire

Hi Donald,

Just had a visit from Copernicus; apparently you are not the centre of the Universe.

> **Doug Clark**
> Currie, Midlothian

SIR – Much as I hate to agree with Trump on any issue, he is right to say that the portrait of him he wants taken down in Colorado's state capital looks nothing like him.

In the painting he doesn't look orange and actually looks sane.

> **John Kennedy**
> Hornchurch, Essex

The Great British giveaway

SIR – Upon hearing the news that the UK is to hand over the Chagos Islands to Mauritius, I expressed concern over the future of Diego Garcia (home to a UK/US military base). My wife was rather puzzled and asked why I was so concerned over the fate of a footballer.

>**Simon Cook**
>Sutton, Surrey

SIR – If Labour gives up the Falkland Islands and Gibraltar as well as the Chagos Islands, would that constitute a triple Lammy?

>**Andrew Babington**
>Portrush, Co Antrim, Northern Ireland

SIR – Let's hope Mr Putin doesn't start taking a fancy to the Isle of Wight.

>**Bob Stebbings**
>Chorleywood, Hertfordshire

SIR – Remove the G for government in Chagos and you have a succinct analysis of our current foreign policy.

>**Hugh Monro**
>Stratton, Cornwall

SIR – I would be delighted to purchase Keir Starmer's home. I only wonder how much he would pay me for taking it.

John Ralph
Henley-on-Thames, Oxfordshire

SIR – Has Sir Keir never watched the film *Love Actually*? Could we have Hugh Grant instead, please?

Jonathan Mann
Gunnislake, Cornwall

SIR – Does Sir Keir Starmer think trying to dress like President Zelensky will enhance his street cred abroad?

Can't wait to see his baseball cap when he visits President Trump or the grass skirt in Hawaii.

Rob Mason
Nailsea, North Somerset

SIR – I look east and see a megalomaniac leader of a heavily armed country, surrounded by fawning oligarchs, invading and threatening neighbouring countries. I look west and see a megalomaniac leader of a heavily armed country, surrounded by fawning oligarchs, attacking and threatening neighbouring countries.

I live in a country led by a students' union committee. Should I be worried?

Michael Austin
Abingdon, Oxfordshire

A Nobel cause

SIR – If Barack Obama got a Nobel Peace Prize for becoming the first black American president, shouldn't Donald Trump receive this award for becoming the first orange one?

Hamish McCracken
Newbury, Berkshire

The fight house

SIR – A short video is doing the rounds which shows Presidents Zelensky and Trump sitting in the Oval Office. The former turns to the latter and gives him a hefty right hook. I confess my spirits soared, until I realised it was a product of AI.

Francis Bown
London E3

SIR – If Mr Trump thinks Mr Zelensky lacks democratic legitimacy, just wait until he finds out about Mr Putin.

Donald MacKenzie
Inverness

SIR – As I listen, with dismay, to another announcement from the White House, I've realised this is a new Netflix series based on an undiscovered Philip K. Dick book.

Catherine Farrell
Gosport, Hampshire

SIR – Trump seems not to understand that diplomacy is the art of letting someone have your way.

Will Rumsey
Crowthorne, Berkshire

SIR – I had considered taking language classes in either Russian or Chinese.

However, recent events have led me to believe that American might be a wiser choice.

Tony Bath
Wallingford, Oxfordshire

SIR – A purely hypothetical question: if a major world leader showed conclusive signs that he was clinically insane, how long would it take other world leaders to pluck up the courage to exclude him (or her) from their policy-making processes?

Tony Turner
Baldock, Hertfordshire

SIR – I think we are all now learning what "Trump derangement syndrome" actually means.

John Clezy
Flims Waldhaus, Switzerland

SIR – I am unsure what Trump's problem is but I can guarantee it is hard to pronounce.

Christopher Learmont-Hughes
Caldy, Wirral

SIR – One has to wonder whether too many cheeseburgers have a detrimental effect on mental capacity.

Bill Todd
Whitton, Middlesex

SIR – Surely Donald Trump and J. D. Vance deserve an Oscar for their Oval Office performance as Godfather and Son in their defenestration of Volodymyr Zelensky. The jibe about having no cards to play and the accusations of "disrespect" were pure Brando and Pacino.

Not only that, they were making poor Mr Zelensky an offer he couldn't refuse.

Richard McNeill
Okehampton, Devon

SIR – When Volodymyr Zelensky has his next appointment in the Oval Office he might consider taking all six feet seven inches of Vitali Klitschko, the mayor of Kyiv, with him. I am sure that he would be delighted to give Mr Trump a handshake that he would never forget.

David Ellis
Ellon, Aberdeenshire

SIR – If President Zelensky was a comedian then President Trump is a joke.

Mary Richards
Fowey, Cornwall

SIR – If one of Donald Trump's participants in *The Apprentice* had made such a hash of the Ukraine deal, they would have been walking from the boardroom in the first episode.

Nik Perfitt
Bristol

SIR – Are we underestimating Mr Trump? Could he be the most brilliant KGB agent in history?

Dr J. R. Drummond
Cellardyke, Fife

SIR – In the light of the US president's decision to side with a Russian dictator over his former allies in Europe, I suggest it's high time we asked for the bust of Winston Churchill to be returned to us from the Oval Office.

Suggestions for a replacement are welcome and I'll start: Krusty the clown from *The Simpsons*.

Iain Duffin
Malmesbury, Wiltshire

SIR – MAGA = Make America Go Away...Please, my head hurts.

Trevor Harvey
Woodstock, Oxfordshire

Ode to the special relationship

SIR – *While Trump and Vance*
May look askance
At one brave leader's clothing,
This attitude is
Much eschewed
And looked upon with loathing.

All praise we bring
To Charles your king
For asking Trump to dinner.
With regal guile
The King will smile,
While Trump purrs "I'm a winner".

> **Rose Hayes**
> Dulverton, Somerset

SIR – Palace officials must guard against the possibility that Trump may attend any state banquet, in his honour, cloaked in ermine.

> **Kenneth Preston**
> Royal Hillsborough, County Down

SIR – In the light of his boorish and ill-mannered treatment of President Zelensky, calls for the King to retract his invitation to Donald Trump could be counterproductive.

A better response would be for his arrival to be met by some well-timed British protests, of the "politely" rude variety.

This could involve turning our backs on the president in any public drive-by, wearing fake tans and absurd comb-overs while waving Ukrainian flags, or boycotting McDonald's or KFC for the day.

And can that satirical inflatable balloon of President Trump in a nappy be dusted down and brought out of storage?

John Rattigan
Doveridge, Derbyshire

Trading blows

SIR – Will President Trump's tariffs outlast a free trade lettuce?

Andrew McGrath
Teddington, Middlesex

SIR – Forget about Black Wednesday or Red Monday or even something called a Silver Thursday, we have now got an Orange Wednesday (and most weekdays since, it would appear).

Merry Baskin
Eastleach, Gloucestershire

SIR – The fictional rogue "deal-maker" who is always just one wheeze away from success is known to all Brits as Del Boy.

It looks like he now has a transatlantic rival in Dol Boy.

John Bath
Clevedon, Somerset

SIR – I am old enough to remember the original "Back Britain" campaign from the 1960s. It was backed by a memorable pop song fronted by the inimitable Bruce Forsyth. Perhaps that should be revived too.

A trio of Keir Starmer, Angela Rayner and Rachel Reeves scantily clad and gyrating wildly should be enough to persuade Mr Trump of the error of his ways.

I commend the idea to the House.

> **Colin G. Parker**
> Thame, Oxfordshire

SIR – Look on the bright side; this could be a good time to buy a left-hand drive Rolls Royce.

> **David Gerrard**
> Broadmayne, Dorset

SIR – Will it be a penguin or a seal leading the Heard and McDonald Islands' delegation in negotiations for a better trade deal with America?

> **Simon Baumgartner**
> Barry, Vale of Glamorgan

SIR – Does all peanut butter contain American nuts? Asking for a friend.

> **Lynne Cowley**
> Bagshot, Surrey

SIR – How dare Donald Trump carry out the promises he made in his election campaign. It is outrageous to deliver pledges made while seeking election. No wonder British politicians have nothing to do with such behaviour.

David Saunders
Sidmouth, Devon

Executive dysfunction

SIR – I have long advocated interrupting the supply of large inflatables to the people traffickers in northern France as a key weapon in stopping the flow of illegal immigrants across the Channel. Similarly, I wonder if blocking the sale of black Sharpie pens in the US could staunch the endless output of executive orders by Donald Trump?

Tim Lovett
Claygate, Surrey

SIR – The message is clear. Do not let ANYONE whose surname begins with the three letters TRU anywhere near national financial decisions.

Philip Roy
Whitchurch, Shropshire

SIR – At least Liz Truss had the decency only to wreck the UK economy.

Alaster Gray
Houghton, Cambridgeshire

SIR – The Great Depression started in 1929.

Imitation is said to be the sincerest form of flattery.

President Trump appears to be unwilling to wait until 2029 to create a centenary re-enactment.

Dr Keith Freeman
Lincoln

Waltz through

SIR – I see Mike Waltz, the US national security adviser, complicit in recent military security leaks, has left his post.

Where did he leave it?

Paul Berry
Barnstaple, Devon

SIR – In these dark and threatening days, we should be grateful for any ray of light to brighten our drab, wretched lives. By the mercy of Providence one such ray has been vouchsafed to us: I refer of course to the ongoing spat between Elon Musk and Donald Trump. To watch these two immature man-babies slugging it out on the world's stage must bring unalloyed joy to millions: joy that can only increase as the days go by and they dig their respective holes ever deeper.

Simon Sholl
Oxford

This is how it all ends

SIR – Israel has its air defence system called "Iron Dome". President Trump has decided that the US will have a very similar system which he has named (what else?) "Golden Dome".

One assumes that when the US is attacked, instead of wailing sirens to alert everyone, there will be little golden telephones going "bling-bling".

John Newbury
Warminster, Wiltshire

SIR – My first thought on reading today's article "Kim hypes up North's newest missile 'to rival any other states'" was to question Kim Kardashian's latest media stunt with her daughter North.

I'm not sure which is worse: a rogue dictator or a reality television star with access to missiles.

Tatiana Pole-Carew
London W12

SIR – We could be on the brink of Armageddon but Pharrell Williams has launched a vastly overpriced limited-edition champagne, complete with bow tie and monogram, and Meghan the Direness of Sussex has hedge cuttings in her ice cubes. We can now celebrate the possible end of civilisation in style.

Susy Goodwin
Ware, Hertfordshire

Sleeping with the enemy

SIR – Not wanting to appear desperate, but where do I apply to be honey trapped?

Kelvin Trott
London SW1

Greta persona non grata

SIR – Thanks to Greta Thunberg's "awareness raising" I am aware once more of Greta Thunberg.

Andrew Macdonald Powney
Edinburgh

SIR – Apart from the utter farce and irrelevance of Greta Thunberg's attempts to break the blockade of Gaza, I find it appalling that the UN representative, Francesca Albanese, called on others to follow her example.

This starkly illustrates her feeling and attitude towards Israel.

Or perhaps she wanted others to receive water and free sandwiches?

David Freeman
Barnet, Hertfordshire

Quelle horreur!

SIR – With the appointment of François Bayrou, France has had six prime ministers in Macron's presidency since 2017. Britain has had a mere five prime ministers in that period.

Once again, we have fallen behind the EU. I blame Brexit.

Gary Graves
Richmond, Surrey

SIR – I note with some interest the decision to drop the name HMS Agincourt in favour of HMS Achilles.

Is this an attempt to curry favour with Greece (rather than return the Elgin Marbles) while at the same time avoiding giving offence to France?

I'm not too worried about the former but have always considered that irritating the French was one of the (many) benefits of being English.

David Hallowell
Tadworth, Surrey

SIR – French officials describing the scheme to return illegal immigrants to France as "symbolic" was clearly mistranslated. It should have read "shambolic".

Dr Martin Keech
Bramley, Surrey

SIR – Earlier this week, after sitting in a huge queue waiting to pass through seriously undermanned and evidently slow-working French border controls at the Calais end of Le Shuttle, we missed our scheduled crossing through the Channel Tunnel.

On reaching the UK Border Control booth my wife remarked to the officer: "You would think the French would be over Brexit nine years on" – to which came the good-natured reply: "Madam, they are not over Agincourt and that was six hundred years ago."

Christopher Timbrell
Kington Langley, Wiltshire

SIR – July 14 was Bastille Day in France, while in the United States it was National Nude Day.

That has to tell us something but I am not sure what.

Richard North
Stanford Dingley, Berkshire

They do things differently there

SIR – In the 1980s I flew with Aeroflot, the Soviet Union's state airline. A sullen hatchet-faced flight attendant asked if I wanted lunch. I enquired as to the choice. "You eat it, or you don't," was her reply. Looking back, they were in the vanguard of budget airlines.

Jonathan Yardley
Wolverhampton

SIR – I remember in 1972 being sent (aged thirteen) to accompany my eight-year-old brother on an Iberia flight to Barcelona. The gin and tonic was excellent.

Valentine Guinness
London W12

SIR – I once strutted off a flight, convinced I was radiating effortless charm: smooth flight, crisply folded newspaper, a dignified nod to the crew.

Surely, I was prime "cheerio" material. Instead, the flight attendant gave me a knowing smirk. Odd, I thought. Was I that devastatingly handsome?

No. I was, in fact, trailing an entire airline blanket, firmly tucked into the back of my trousers like some kind of budget superhero cape. No "cheerio" that day – just the unmistakable look of someone who couldn't wait to gossip about 22B.

Yours, tragically,

Richard Rose
London NW4

SIR – My father was a tomato grower, and each season selected a prize specimen of each variety to provide free seeds for the next year's crop.

On retirement, he and my mother emigrated to Australia. On being told that he could not bring tomato seeds into that country, he took three tomatoes, one of each preferred variety, and ate them before boarding the plane.

You can guess the rest.

Philip Roy
Whitchurch, Shropshire

SIR – I have just returned from the Antipodes and wish to complain, in the strongest possible terms, about the chaotic state in which they maintain the firmament down there. I'll start with the moon which is not only upside down but also travels from right to left across the night sky which, as any selenophile can tell you, is simply wrong. The sun isn't quite so bad in that, while it also unfortunately processes from right to left, it is at least the right way up. Finally, the stars are a complete mess and seem to have been scattered randomly across the heavens and, yes you've guessed it, they rotate anticlockwise through the course of the night. Shocking!

James Paxman
Sheffield, South Yorkshire

SIR – Having been to 110 countries it is clear to me that civilisation ends at Dover (with the possible exception of New Zealand, which is invariably closed), that God is an Englishman and that when one dies one doesn't go to heaven but to Yorkshire. The overspill goes to Devon.

Tony Davis
Hallaton, Leicestershire

TRAVELLING
HOPEFULLY

Surfaces may be slippery

SIR – You report that members of the Aslef rail union refused to walk to their trains after it snowed in the night.

In a spirit of solidarity and comradeship, can I just warn all staff that in months to come the warmer weather may reappear, bringing a risk of sunburn, heatstroke or just general enjoyment of life.

Best to put your head in a SPF200 saucepan and hide behind the sofa (or loaf on it).

Antony Thomas
Esher, Surrey

SIR – The Aslef train drivers could have safely walked to work across the snow if they had followed NHS Scotland's advice to "walk like penguins". Advice on how to do this is readily available online.

Dr C. D. E. Morris
Walsall, Staffordshire

Public service announcement

SIR – My favourite train announcement was travelling from Manchester approaching the base of the Deputy Prime Minister Angela Rayner. "Next stop Brinnington… if you are getting out here – good luck."

T. Lowe
Manchester

SIR – As part of a barbershop quartet, and dressed as a giant banana, I was involved in being filmed on hidden camera for the launch of the BBC's digital channels.

Oxford station was one of the locations, unbeknown to the station authorities. Within minutes of covert filming starting, a public address announcement was made: "Would passengers on platform one awaiting the London train please be careful to avoid slipping on banana skins."

David Proud
Lambourn, Berkshire

SIR – Many years ago, I was sitting on a local service train in Nottingham station waiting to depart. Watching other trains coming in and then leaving, people were becoming increasingly restless. Eventually the train guard announced over the tannoy: "I do apologise for the late departure of this service, but it is due to a typical British Rail cock-up." Hysterical laughter ensued, removing all tension.

Margaret Baker
Juvigny les Vallées, Manche, France

The struggle is rail

SIR – You report that a group of travellers moved onto a greenbelt field, cleared over six acres of land, built a ten-foot-high security fence around it, bulldozed it level, spread stone, topped it with gravel and moved thirteen caravans and a variety of other vehicles onto it, all in 72 hours. Clearly the Government should offer them the contract to build HS2; they could have it completed and trains running by Christmas, and then build the third runway at Heathrow ready for Easter.

Len Tabner
High Boulby, North Yorkshire

SIR – I am a regular traveller on both First Great Western and South Western trains. Both companies refund part or all of my ticket if the train is more than 15 minutes late.

I wonder how much compensation the Nasa astronauts, who thought that they would be back on Earth eight days later, are entitled to receive from Boeing after a nine-month delay.

Robin Thomas
Exeter, Devon

SIR – Taking advantage of the reduced rate for seniors, I recently went interrailing around Austria and Germany. Every train was either cancelled or arrived half an hour late.

My travel would have been a lot easier if I'd had a 15-year-old with a smartphone doing the rescheduling.

Dr John Doherty
Stratford-upon-Avon, Warwickshire

SIR – To demolish the Government's case for renationalising the railways of this country, I suggest just five words: "Remember the British Rail sandwich".

Dr Michael Young
Winterbourne Dauntsey, Wiltshire

SIR – On one train journey I endured a chap's loud, disruptive phone conversation, during which he read out his number to someone. I enjoyed the next half hour ringing his number numerous times until became so annoyed, he switched off his mobile. Fun and peace all round.

Dudley Swain
Exeter, Devon

SIR – I read with delight your article about the train taken over by squirrels, which was ultimately closed down and returned to base.

I have had the misfortune to watch several episodes of the ghastly *Nightsleeper*. This has panicking travellers running from carriage to carriage and implacable villains seeking unknown outcomes. So does the squirrel train, but the plot is far superior, with a trained squad armed with brooms, litter pickers and peanuts deployed to counter the terrorist threat.

More please.

I hesitate to add that male travellers should have been advised to tuck their trousers into their socks in case the squirrels were trained to go for the nuts.

Gray Pratt
Banchory, Aberdeenshire

Where to stop?

SIR – You have no comprehension of how relieved
I was to hear that Transport for London has finally
come to its senses and banned book exchange shelves
on the London Underground. These blatant fire
hazards have been a risk to life and limb for far too
long.

As "combustible material", books are clearly
dangerous and should not be tolerated in public
spaces. I am sure that all right-thinking people (of
which there are far too many, including the Mayor
of London) will agree with me that, in order to save
innocent commuters unnecessary exposure to danger,
the carrying of individual books on the Tube should
also now be banned. And briefcases. And posters.
And wigs. And clothes.

It is for the greater good.

Giles Ramsay
London SW17

The absolute limit

SIR – It was good to read that a future Tour de France
will include stages in Scotland, England and Wales.

Has anybody told the organisers that most villages,
towns and cities in Wales have a 20mph speed limit?

Roger W. Payne
Chelford, Cheshire

SIR – It seems there is little evidence that 20mph speed limits in Wales have resulted in a reduction of accidents. I wonder what rules the government will introduce next.

Have they researched the number of men who fall over when pulling on their underpants and trousers, hitting their heads on bedside tables? Could the introduction of kilts be an answer?

Michael Cattell
Mollington, Cheshire

Show on the road

SIR – I wish to declare yesterday, April 27, Convertible Day 2025: the first Sunday in the year when every driver of a convertible car can get the hood down and drive along with a fixed smile, wisps of hair blowing in the breeze.

I had a Mini convertible for a short time in the 1980s, but its hood was stolen overnight. My wife-to-be and I searched the streets and front gardens of Crouch End in vain, saying we were looking for a lost cat if anyone asked what we were doing.

David Miller
Tunbridge Wells, Kent

SIR – The number of DeLorean cars registered with the DVLA fails to account for the high number of DeLorean cars currently being driven in the future and the past.

Unfortunately, the DVLA has no method of quantifying this number.

Mark Carver-Smith
Barwell, Leicestershire

SIR – In the event of total destruction following a nuclear war I have been led to believe over the years that only the likes of ants, cockroaches and termites would survive. I am not a scientist but believe that should Armageddon occur in this manner, taxis and Amazon Prime vans would also survive.

Tim Rann
Mirfield, West Yorkshire

SIR – If one is considering a second-hand electric car, is there any way to tell whether it is pre-loved or pre-loathed?

John Williams
Bradwell-on-Sea, Essex

Test of another time

SIR – I had driving lessons in the 1970s when miniskirts were in fashion. My instructor's advice for my test was "wear your shortest skirt". I had a female examiner, but I did pass first time.

Wendy Tibbetts
Halesowen, West Midlands

SIR – After several years of marriage my father encouraged my mother to take her driving test, which she failed three times. At the fourth attempt the examiner asked why this was the case and her reply was: "Well, each time my husband brought out the L-plates I became pregnant and couldn't fit behind the wheel". She passed.

Bryony Hill
Hurstpierpoint, West Sussex

SIR – My wife's grandmother was of the generation who never needed to take a test. She surmounted her own limitations by always asking that her cars, when being prepared to leave the local garage, be parked "facing Inverness".

Andrew Wauchope
London SE11

SIR – A friend was very concerned about his elderly father's ability to drive. He suggested that on his father's next visit to his GP, he should ask the doctor's advice. Asking his father later if he had mentioned driving to the doctor, his father said the doctor had queried whether he was quick enough to perform an emergency stop. "Oh yes," his father had replied: "I'm doing those all the time."

> **Jackie Atwell**
> Felbridge, Surrey

SIR – A friend once hired a car in France. Try as he might he could not engage reverse gear.

Frustrated, he wound down the window and called out to a somewhat startled passer-by: *"Madame, j'ai oublié mon derrière."*

> **David Vigar**
> Sedbergh, Cumbria

SIR – In the early 1960s I was working as a trainee mechanic in my local garage. The MOT system had only recently been introduced and, at the time, it was only for cars over ten years old. You can imagine the quality and state of some of the cars that came in for testing. The foreman, and MOT tester, was ex-military and could often be heard chastising the customers: "The war's over now sir, we can stop your car headlights looking for enemy bombers."

> **Christopher Bocock**
> Quorn, Leicestershire

You have reached your destination

SIR – It was interesting to read of the 25,000 streets of London that cabbies are expected to know. I used to visit a client in Bleeding Heart Yard, just behind Hatton Garden and often had to give the cabbie precise directions. That was until one cabbie, who knew where to go, explained to me that the Yard was so named because it was "bleeding hard to find it!"

Michael Draper
Nether Wallop, Hampshire

SIR – While out walking I once persuaded my dear wife to stand next to a road nameplate, as I usually take a photo as a memento of a pleasant visit.

When I showed her the photo some time later, she realised that she had been "set up", although fortunately her sense of humour did not let her down. The name of the road was Dumb Woman's Lane.

We are still happily married after 48 years.

Clive Goddard
Bexhill-on-Sea, East Sussex

SIR – Driving to Ulcombe yesterday evening, I passed the end of Pleasure House Lane; on balance, I felt it best I keep on going.

Peter Hall
Marden, Kent

SIR – Driving through Newport, Shropshire I always look forward to seeing what is going on in Frolic Street. So far I have been disappointed: not a jester, stilt-walker or acrobat troupe in sight.

Not even a one-man band. However, I remain hopeful.

Sheila Taylor
Cardigan, Ceredigion

Notes on a small island

SIR – An American friend of mine returned from a visit to Cornwall and commented that the hotel plumbing was older than the American Constitution, and when a plaque stated that the building dated from 959 the I was not missing from the front.

He was also pleased to see that people in Cornwall do not carry guns.

Professor Tim Connell
Esher, Surrey

SPORTING
TRIUMPH AND
DISASTER

Worn to win

SIR – Do false nails and false eyelashes really make women athletes run faster?

> **Jane Bubb**
> Esher, Surrey

SIR – I admire David Beckham, but clip-on braces are a no-no.

> **Ashley Preston**
> Shipley, West Sussex

SIR – Is David Beckham to be knighted for services to the tattoo industry?

> **Geoff Fleming**
> Heytesbury, Wiltshire

SIR – With the award of a knighthood to Gareth Southgate for getting England to the final stages of a major tournament, should Thomas Tuchel be successful in actually winning something then surely canonisation or at the very least beatification will be on the cards.

> **John Sharp**
> Farnham, Surrey

SIR – The hard way to get a gong is helping others, less lucky than yourself, for a long time. The easiest way is to be extremely well paid for what you do and become a multimillionaire. However, it transpires that there is one even easier way: playing darts.

You must excuse me – I'm off to the pub.

> **Robert Pugh**
> Llandeilo, Carmarthenshire

Boy and girls come out to play

SIR – With the current transgender row raging across sport, I see no rule preventing biological women playing against men. Following the England men's abject performances over the last few days, there must be a strong case for replacing them with the Lionesses.

John Roberts
Wokingham, Berkshire

SIR – As a former inhabitant of Newmarket, and now living in Lambourn, I have been having a little chat with one or two racing colts, and they are considering taking my suggestion and identifying as fillies, so as to be able to carry less weight in major races.

Nicky Samengo-Turner
Lambourn, Berkshire

SIR – The solution to cricket's transgender problem is for those players to form their own side and call themselves Middlesex.

Michael Knox
Beaconsfield, Buckinghamshire

One giant leap

SIR - Your article commenting on Jonathan Edwards' 30-year triple jump world record highlighted an amazing achievement. Thirty five years before this milestone, I competed in schoolboy events performing the less glamorously titled "hop, step and jump".

Rather a trivial title and not a terribly popular event. I take pride, however, in showing off my third place certificate in a county schoolboy event.
I don't usually mention that there were only three competitors.

William Freeman
East Molesey, Surrey

Eyes on the ball

SIR – If the England football team are looking for a new manager, they need look no further than the *Match of the Day* pundit Alan Shearer. When he is commenting on football matches he always knows exactly what has gone wrong and how it should be done instead. It would also save the BBC a lot of money.

Adrian Insall
Royston, Hertfordshire

SIR – I suggest the correct solution to clue 10 Across (6), in Sunday's prize Cryptic No. 3,283 (Those that beat Scottish football team) is "anyone".

Paul Earl
Helsinki, Finland

SIR – After snatching victory from the jaws of defeat twice – against Sweden and Italy – the Lionesses should be renamed the Houdinis, after the great American escapologist Harry Houdini. And their victory song *Sweet Caroline* should be replaced by the Rolling Stones' *19th Nervous Breakdown*.

> **Stan Labovitch**
> Windsor, Berkshire

SIR – Could someone please ask the Lionesses to try and score their equalising and winning goals a little earlier. Their last two games certainly made for a very exciting football match, but I am 82 years old and my blood pressure tablets are having to work overtime.

> **Barry Smith**
> Frodsham, Cheshire

SIR – To paraphrase Dorothy Parker, "Men seldom raise glasses to girls who miss passes" – an aphorism which the gloriously victorious Lionesses need never fear.

> **John Holm Gray**
> Goring-on-Thames, Oxfordshire

And the crowd goes wild

SIR – Learning that celebration of last weekend's Premiership-sealing goals against Tottenham Hotspur produced Earth tremors peaking at 1.74 on the Richter scale, I would like to be assured that Liverpool FC will henceforth be permanently banned.

Dr Robert Linden F. Kay
Wantage, Oxfordshire

SIR – A footballer scores a goal, rips off his shirt and runs bare torso around the pitch; you cover this with great gusto, two photographs over two pages.

I am a quantity surveyor and if I successfully calculate a quantity I don't feel the need to similarly run around the building site. What if we all did this?

Jonathan Yardley
Wolverhampton

SIR – One Twickenham rugby match day, I was putting my young daughter to bed when we heard a very drunken rendition of "Swing Low" coming from the street outside. "I thought Daddy was at home," she said.

Emma-Louise Bowers
London SW11

A case of the Oxford blues

SIR – What excess of wokery persuaded the BBC to describe the Oxford Boat Race crew as "runners-up"? With an average age of 25, these stalwarts are no longer in kindergarten, nor do they require to be treated as such.

However regrettable it may have been to those of us of a Dark Blue persuasion, the plain fact is they lost.

William Gunn
Hereford

Technical fault

SIR – With the replacement of line judges at Wimbledon with electronic gadgets, why not go the whole hog and replace the players with AI and robotic creations? Just think – there would be no more tantrums, obsessive demands for new balls, towels or drinks. Wouldn't it be fun?

Grenville Edwards
Albaston, Cornwall

SIR – I was hoping that with the spread of AI we would soon be able to watch tennis with the commentary but without the extreme grunting noises from some of the players which make some matches impossible to sit through.

Sadly technology has not yet advanced for this, so it's back to relying on the volume control.

Brian Storey
Cambridge

SIR – I wonder how all the tennis fans at Wimbledon manage to cope without two or three commentators explaining what's going on.

Ian Stearn
Chichester, West Sussex

SIR – A British duo won the men's doubles at Wimbledon for the first time in more than 80 years.

They must both be incredibly fit if they have been playing tennis that long!

Dave Bassett
Liverpool

Howzat?

SIR – Watching recent TV coverage of a match at Lord's, viewers witnessed at least two solar panels destroyed by a cricket ball. To help minimise our carbon footprint, should batsmen be stopped from hitting sixes?

Michael Nicholson
Newton Abbot, Devon

SIR – The great Ben Stokes said on radio that the tight Test match against India was "*literally* cat and mouse". How can we defeat the abuse of the word literally? It literally makes me explode.

Brian Emsley
Newmarket, Suffolk

En route to victory

SIR – I've watched most of the first four stages of the Tour de France covering about 750 kilometres, and I've yet to see a pothole.

Not surprisingly the word is not in my pocket French dictionary.

David Bristow
Tunbridge Wells, Kent

The next round

SIR – Following Rory McIlroy's triumph in The Masters, I await President Trump's announcement that he is introducing tariffs on incoming foreign golfers in order to encourage home-grown talent and Make America Great Again.

Geoffrey Boyd
Fowey, Cornwall

SIR – It is a pity this year's Ryder Cup is "over there". If it were "here" the perfect way to retaliate against tariffs imposed by the US on the EU and UK would be to put a 10 per cent surcharge on American team scores. They score in the 60s, we add 6 to their card. In the 70s, add 7. This virtually guarantees a European win.

Kim Thonger
Collyweston, Northamptonshire

SIR – Should consideration be given to nationalising all foreign-owned golf courses in Scotland?

Michael Davies
Tatworth, Somerset

Great Scottie

SIR – With his in-depth understanding of mashies and niblicks, how to approach greens in so many different ways and a speciality of toad-in-the-hole-in-one, it was no surprise to me that this year's British Open Golf Championship was won by the Scottish chef.

David Channon
Bury, Lancashire

What I really, really don't want

SIR – I am dismayed and alarmed at the decision by Red Bull to sack Christian Horner.

It's not that I am a fan of F1, far from it. But if Horner and his wife Geri Halliwell find themselves short of money, the Spice Girls may release a new single, or worse, reform for a tour.

I urge Red Bull to reconsider.

Kathie Glennon
Whickham, Tyne and Wear

THAT'S
ENTERTAINMENT

All about the drama

SIR – There's a desperate need to reopen the Nottinghamshire pits or cover the North Sea with turbines. Only continuous power cuts can explain why no one in *Sherwood* has a lit house or even tries the light switch when they enter a room.

R. Allan Reese
Dorchester, Dorset

SIR – I have noticed that in many TV police dramas, solicitors accompanying suspects in interrogation rooms never utter a word.

Although I have never acted in my life, I am thinking of applying for my Equity card.

Mike Bingham
Alvechurch, Worcestershire

Out of time (and space)

SIR – I watched the first episode of *Doctor Who* on Saturday 23 November 1963. I have willed him on in most of the decades since. Now that the Doctor has regenerated well beyond a Time Lord's allocated number of selves, it is time – just this once – for Daleks to triumph and exterminate him/her/them.

Charles Foster
Chalfont St Peter, Buckinghamshire

Back to reality

SIR – In the early 1960s, I appeared as a Yeoman extra in Gilbert & Sullivan's *The Yeoman of the Guard*, staged in the moat of the Tower of London as part of the City's arts festival (in front of the late Queen and broadcast on BBC TV).

I wonder if I am thus qualified to appear in any celebrity editions of popular TV quiz shows, or as a celebrity contestant in any reality TV competition. My qualifications surely compete favourably with most of the others currently featured in such shows.

> **Robert Anthony**
> Croydon, Surrey

SIR – The Saturday night lineup for BBC 1 is *The Weakest Link, Pointless Celebrities* and *Casualty*. That just about sums it up.

> **Jane Eyles**
> Mahon, Menorca

SIR – On Saturday I promised my wife that I would not pass any adverse comments or sigh and moan while she watched *Strictly Come Dancing.* I kept my promise. I fell asleep.

> **Derrick G. Smith**
> Bexhill-on-Sea, East Sussex

SIR – The singer Gladness Jukic claims that the BBC stole her reality show idea.

I am an amateur wood turner and I think wood turning would be an ideal craft to add to the many skill-based competitions that are being aired. Let me put it on public record that *The Great British Turn-Off* is my idea and the broadcasters will need my consent to develop it.

Peter Hatherell
Melksham, Wiltshire

SIR – I'd love to see Victoria Beckham and Stella McCartney competing on *The Great British Sewing Bee.*

D. Derbyshire
Northwich, Cheshire

Farming today

SIR – The US election result surprised me, but such is life.

However, a storyline on *The Archers* being dominated by AI is surely a step too far.

Neil Stuart
Tavistock, Devon

SIR – With the cricket season approaching, I wonder if it is time for *The Archers* to employ a cricket adviser as well as an agricultural one.

It would save cricketers up and down the country shouting at the radio in frustration at some of the ludicrous story lines.

I will offer favourable terms.

Steve Donlan
Saltburn-by-the-Sea, North Yorkshire

BBC's kitchen nightmare

SIR – It would seem that many of those responsible for the production of *MasterChef* failed to take appropriate action despite multiple reports of improper language being used by both presenters. If the new series is to be broadcast perhaps a more fitting title would be *MainlyDeaf.*

Stuart Harrington
Burnham-on-Sea, Somerset

Variations on a theme

SIR – With several months to go before the start of the BBC Proms, there is stiff competition between the BBC Radio 3 presenters to see who can squeeze in the most plugs for it.

My licence fee is on Tom "The Prom" McKinney, who serves it up thick and fast on the breakfast show. Tom Service must be respected as no one else can cram so many words into one sentence, but Sarah Walker could still pinch it with a late gush.

Kevin Murphy
Blacksnape, Lancashire

SIR – Last night of the Proms, and there's Keir Starmer playing his own trumpet. I closed the sitting room door to keep the hot air in.

Adrian Johnston
Rugby, Warwickshire

When will there be good news?

SIR – I recently recorded the film *Apocalypse Now*.

When I came to watch it, I found it depressingly full of doom and gloom, and it was a while before I realised I had put on the BBC *News at Six* by accident.

Rupert Godfrey
Heytesbury, Wiltshire

SIR – A trigger warning for *News at Ten*:

Caution: the next 30 minutes might feature, or contain references to, President Trump.

Roger Ward
London N1

SIR – Trying to extract some clarity from last night's *Question Time*, I found myself wondering if it might be improved by renaming it *Answer Time*.

Kip Calderara
Chesham, Buckinghamshire

Fame and fortune

SIR – With every episode of *The Martin Lewis Money Show*, I am realising that this genius could crash the economy on his own.

We must look after our future Chancellor of the Exchequer.

Nigel Lines
Ferndown, Dorset

Serenading Europe

SIR – The Prime Minister must be so busy plotting his capitulation to EU demands that he's forgotten to blame the Tories for our receiving *nul points* in the Eurovision public vote.

Lisa Dumbavand
London SW18

SIR – Top of Keir Starmer's must-haves in his discussions with the EU should be a guarantee that for the next five years the UK Eurovision entry will receive *douze points* from a minimum of four EU national votes, otherwise *pas d'accord*.

John Doonan
Kirknewton, West Lothian

SIR – I watched the Eurovision Song Contest with the sound turned down. This provided an acceptable silent stage version of Cirque du Soleil.

Keith Davies
Telford, Shropshire

The final whistle for Gary Lineker

SIR – Now that Gary Lineker is finally leaving the BBC perhaps he will have some time on his hands. Studying for a GCSE in Modern History may be a useful start.

Linda Willby
Thornton Le Dale, North Yorkshire

SIR – Finally, a VAR outcome welcomed by the long-suffering supporters of the BBC.

Annie Bennett
Oving, West Sussex

SIR – Thankfully we no longer need to listen to the preacher known locally as "The Cheese & Onion Kid". My licence fee suddenly becomes much better value.

Clive Kellett
Slough, Berkshire

Rock of ages

SIR – In the 1960s I went to Eel Pie Island to see rhythm and blues singer Long John Baldry. In the shadow of his act was a slight figure very much on his own and seemingly ignored. I asked who it was. Rod Stewart, came the answer. Without even hearing him sing, my teenage opinion was decisive. "Such a shame. He'll never make it." Apologies, Sir Rod. Glastonbury was great.

Margaret Staveley-Wadham
Little Bognor, West Sussex

SIR – On the way into the Glastonbury Festival site we are greeted by a large sign that announces the site to be a "drone-free zone", yet on Friday afternoon they gave Caroline Lucas a microphone and access to the Pyramid Stage.

David Amos
Stockton on Tees, Co Durham

SIR – It's difficult to know what the punk rap duo Bob Vylan want out of life apart from killing the rich – which would mean no more Premier League football players or headline acts at Glastonbury. Their greatest crime is adapting the name of Bob Dylan, the internationally loved singer-songwriter, for which there is no forgiveness.

Brian Cole
Robertsbridge, East Sussex

More questions asked

SIR – The new series of *Mastermind, Only Connect* and *University Challenge* can mean only one thing – the approach of winter. How depressing.

Penny Adie
Morebath, Devon

God rest ye merry salesmen

SIR – If the Chancellor only slapped a tax on Christmas TV adverts broadcast before December 1, the country would be solvent by the New Year.

Peter Lilley
West Hallam, Derbyshire

SIR – After studying this year's TV Christmas ads, I am forced to conclude that the average British actor spends three years at Rada, memorises 30 Shakespeare plays and braves stage fright and hostile critics simply to utter once a year the words "succulent British turkey".

Jim Gibb
Newcastle upon Tyne

SIR – I hate watching advertisements on TV. The only one I like ends with "keep away from children at all times".

Ian Hunt
Ferndown, Dorset

Best of British

SIR – I was pleased to hear that Amazon had bought the James Bond franchise and am looking forward to seeing Jeremy Clarkson as 007.

Denise Burningham
Newton Abbot, Devon

SIR – How on earth did Paddington Bear get that passport photograph past the issuing authority? He obviously didn't read the instructions. Among other things, you must be looking straight at the camera, your mouth must be closed and both eyes must be visible. At least he has removed his headwear (and any concealed marmalade sandwich).

Clearly, there's one rule for national treasures and another for the rest of us.

Hilary Aitken
Kilmacolm, Renfrewshire

Trigger happy

SIR – Last night I was watching professional boxing on television. I was shocked to learn, via a trigger warning announcement, that the programme "may contain violence".

I would have been very disappointed indeed had this not been the case.

Charles Dobson
Burton in Kendal, Cumbria

SIR – I have just succeeded in acquiring tickets for the new production of *Much Ado About Nothing*, coming to the Theatre Royal, Drury Lane, starring Tom Hiddleston and Hayley Atwell.

Much to my surprise during the course of the booking process I was advised that "there is a mild threat of violence and misogyny and some sexual content."

Was ever a production more aptly named?

Ian Joseph
London N3

SIR – I have recently seen a play that portrays child neglect and cruelty, racial stereotyping, glorification of criminality and male-on-female violence.

Despite the fact there were no trigger warnings, my wife and I greatly enjoyed *Oliver!* at Chichester Theatre.

Jeremy Hamilton-Miller
Nottingham

THE RIGHT ROYALS

Hair apparent

SIR – The reported reaction of Princess Charlotte to her first sight of her father's apology for a beard indicates that she is a young lady of discernment and taste.

Michael Ellwood
Painswick, Gloucestershire

The Sussex test

SIR – My 89-year-old father is no fan of the Duchess of Sussex. His daily despair at the inevitable articles about her in the paper is a source of great amusement (to me). However recently, after suffering a seizure, he was in the postictal state. Seeking to entertain him I turned on *With Love, Meghan*, telling him cheerily: "You can see what all the fuss is about". To my amazement he truly enjoyed it. The following morning I thought I would repeat the experience with episode two, but after a couple of minutes he shut the iPad cover, saying "This is absolute nonsense". The postictal state was over.

I suggested to the doctors that this might be a superb way of establishing brain function in future patients.

Claudia van der Werff
London SW1

SIR – I see that the Duchess of Sussex has shared a picture of herself preparing a meal over the weekend.

I've done the same, if anyone's interested.

Graham Fish
Hertford

Jam tomorrow

SIR – Please could someone tell me what Prince Harry does all day – hull strawberries perhaps?

> **Roger Job**
> Worcester

SIR – I've been trying to draw some parallels between Meghan's "As Ever" Montecito raspberry spread and my "Oh Not Again" gooseberry jam, prepared from our own home-grown fruit. While mine also "shows care to the people in my life", I'd be hard pressed to attract a wider market with the slogan that it will "mimic the magic of Chesterfield".

> **Janet Dillon**
> Chesterfield, Derbyshire

SIR – One item that I believe the Duchess of Sussex should immediately add to her "As Ever" range are sick bags. They could become her number one best seller.

> **Steve Boyden**
> Leatherhead, Surrey

Spare us

SIR – Some 60 years ago, when I was in London, an Australian friend used to tell me that when a jumbo jet landed at Sydney airport, you could tell if it was from the UK, because when the pilot turned the jet engines off, the whining noise continued.

I was reminded of this on seeing the interview with Prince Harry on television the other day. I turned the TV off half way through, but I am sure I could hear the whining noise continuing.

Hamish Watson
Marlborough, Wiltshire

SIR – Meghan and Harry remind me of teeth. Ignore them and they'll go away.

Dr P. E. Pears
Coleshill, Warwickshire

Acceptable damages

SIR – Will you please hack my telephones? My rates are very reasonable, a snip at £50,000. Of course, I would not ask were I still young enough to kick a football around a field.

Michael Messam
Swindon, Wiltshire

A queen's ransom

SIR – I see that the cost of the proposed memorial to the late Queen will be £46 million. Is it going to be built by lawyers?

> **Peter Bull**
> Hope Valley, Derbyshire

I spy another scandal

SIR – I am not surprised that Prince Andrew is being castigated for not realising he was being taken for a ride by an alleged Chinese spy.

It should have been obvious immediately as he would have been wearing a long mac, false nose and moustache and carrying under his coat a round football-shaped object with the word BOMB written on it.

Everybody knows that!

> **Trevor Fielding**
> Oldham, Lancashire

SIR – Are the security arrangements at the home of Prince Andrew in place to keep the baddies out or to keep him in?

> **Vincent Hearne**
> Chinon, Centre-Val de Loire, France

USE AND ABUSE
OF LANGUAGE

S-P-E-L-L it out

SIR – My grandson is about to begin his degree course at Cambridge and he has been allotted a room in College. The brochure offers a "chest of draws" in the bedroom; in the shared kitchen there is a "single freezer draw".

Memory tells me that when I arrived at Girton College in 1966 we all knew how to spell *drawer*, but in those days we had to have Latin at O level.

Elizabeth Jones
Ashford, Kent

Let them be clear

SIR – A new verb has entered the parliamentary lexicon: "to starmer [verb – no object] – to evade and prevaricate at the despatch box with the acquiescence of the Speaker in order to avoid answering the question. Not to be confused with: to lammy [verb – never any object] – to bloviate, to gibber at length."

P.J. Carroll
London SW17

SIR – Would the Prime Minister please stop taking decisions, if only because we don't know where he takes them. On the other hand I am interested in the decisions he makes.

Colin Hamilton
Chichester, West Sussex

SIR – I believe the term "managed decline" to be disingenuous. Under Tory and Labour governments there has been little management about it.

David Lott
Storrington, West Sussex

SIR – Perhaps someone could explain the difference between a "clusterf---" and an "omnishambles". I think we need to know as it's likely both will be needed a lot in the next four years and I wouldn't want to get it wrong.

K. Nesbitt
Ramsey, Isle of Man

SIR – Can someone please inform our Chancellor that it is impossible to fill a black hole, and anything that goes in cannot come out again.

Sheila Hardman
Stockport, Cheshire

SIR – If I hear "£22 billion black hole", "hard-working families", "our NHS", or, worst of all, "only 500 farms" again, I could well find myself committing a non-crime hate incident against a middle-class son of a toolmaker.

Nick Kester
Wattisfield, Suffolk

SIR – We've seen DOGE but Britain needs DONC, the Department of New Cliches. Let's have a laser-like focus on iron-clad rules for new cliches to be deployed by the Government. The users, of course, would be "Donceys".

Colin Moore
Whitehill, Hampshire

SIR – While Sir Keir Starmer's efforts to galvanize our European neighbours in support of Ukraine are admirable, I do wish he had come up with a punchier name. Faced with loutish Trump and ruthless Putin, "coalition of the willing" sounds like an afternoon knitting circle.

Dominic Weston Smith
Faringdon, Oxfordshire

What the doctors ordered

SIR – I note that "junior" doctors now want to be referred to as "resident" doctors. I would like to suggest that we stay with the original designation on the basis that they are proving to be extremely childish.

Nigel Austen
Cirencester, Gloucestershire

SIR – I see that NHS doctors have been given an AI assistant that frees up their time with patients by making notes during appointments. The system being trialled is called Tortus. Isn't this name a hostage to fortune?

Chris King
Woking, Surrey

When black is white

SIR – In view of the recent police instruction not to use the term *blacklisted*, may I suggest that all menus are now shorn of *whitebait*?

Duncan Christie-Miller
Teddington, Middlesex

SIR – If various police forces are being instructed to consider phrases like "black sheep" to be unacceptable, how can a farmer report sheep rustling from his or her Black Welsh Mountain flock?

Max Coventry
Compton Abdale, Gloucestershire

There may be trouble ahead

SIR – Does the train announcer at Clapham Junction know something we don't when he announces the time of the next train to War Minister?

Geraldine Marling-Roberts
Lymington, Hampshire

Very good, Sir

SIR – The month of May and thus the beginning of
the entertaining season has arrived, witnessed by the
incongruous sight of nine uniformed butlers waiting
on our rural station platform yesterday en route to
the livery halls of the City of London. I couldn't help
asking them what the collective noun might be for
such a group. The senior among them said there were
some frankly boring descriptions of a "staff" or a
"retinue", but their preference was to be known as a
"lush" of butlers. What ho!

Nick Crean
Marlborough, Wiltshire

Spread the words

SIR – The greatest word in English must be *nefarious*.
When I was the head of my school's science fiction
club, I would try to get it into every weekly bulletin
of our activities. Credit to the school's head boy who
always struggled manfully to make sense of it all when
reading the announcements during assembly.

Robert Frazer
Salford, Lancashire

SIR – One of my favourite words is *pusillanimity*, but
I've never had the courage to try to say it.

Huw Baumgartner
Bridell, Pembrokeshire

SIR – For some years I have been trying to find an occasion for using the word *nympholepsy* (the frenzied pursuit of the unattainable). Perhaps this letter …?

Michael Allisstone
Chichester, West Sussex

Is it just US?

SIR – Going forward, I trust that Simon Heffer will reach out to those impacted by the Americanisation of English, or, at least, in time contact those affected by it.

Charles Lewis
London N2

SIR – To my mind the only people who should be using the term "reach out" are the Four Tops.

Ian Fraser
Swindon, Wiltshire

SIR – Several years ago my CEO, based in the US, rang me at home one evening to discuss a decision which I had made earlier in the day and with which he disagreed. We conversed for some time before he told me he was "pissed". Obviously, I thought, it was his inebriation making him so strident. I told him not to worry and we could review this the next day. A few sentences later I was under no illusion that it was with my decision he, in his sobriety, was "pissed off".

John Edmondson
Ferndown, Dorset

Quite a mouthful

SIR – I agree with Susie Dent's article about the unnecessary language used on menus. Am I alone in being disturbed, and not just by the spelling, of anything prepared in the "chef's own jus"?

Mark Robbins
Bruton, Somerset

SIR – I fondly remember a menu on which the roast beef was said to be "escorted" by roast potatoes, seasonal vegetables and Yorkshire pudding.

Derek Wellman
Lincoln

Reports on the ground

SIR – Why do weather forecast presenters say, "It's raining out there"? Is it a warning to those with leaky roofs?

Harriet Crocker
Bristol

SIR – It is difficult to overestimate the number of media interviewees who say *underestimate* when they mean *overestimate*.

Gordon Brown
Grassington, North Yorkshire

SIR – Zoe Strimpel is to be congratulated on getting her subjects to toe the line. The fashion these days is to *tow* it.

D. Gibson
Letchworth, Hertfordshire

SIR – I would like to echo Simon Heffer's belief in the importance of the semicolon. Three years ago, it was found that I had developed bowel cancer. Very soon after, I had part of my large intestine removed and since then my reliance on a semicolon has been self-evident.

Grant Jordan
Basingstoke, Hampshire

Lost in translation

SIR – The Latin motto on the coat of arms of a good friend is *Procede Cor Fortis* – which he tells me means "Lead on, Brave Heart".

However, he adds that when the Latin is translated into Japanese, the answer comes forth as "Heart Attack Follows".

Gordon Casely
Crathes, Kincardineshire

SIR – I downloaded a form, in French, to apply for a
Crit'Air sticker for driving in French cities' clean air
zones. Not speaking French too well I translated the
form into English and filled it in. I then translated
it back to French and submitted it. To keep a copy, I
then translated the French back to English only to find
that AI had translated my first name, Peter, literally. I
am now known as To Fart Gamble (look it up).

Peter Gamble
Sainte-Ramée, Nouvelle-Aquitaine, France

If memory serves

SIR – While swotting for my law conversion exams, I
came up with many inventive mnemonics to help with
learning case law and statutes. Now, twenty years later,
although I can remember the mnemonics, I have no
idea what they stand for.

Philip Womack
London NW1

SIR – While studying human anatomy during my
undergraduate training in dentistry I learnt many
useful mnemonics to help remember the order of the
cranial nerves, the branches of the external carotid
artery and many others.

I still remember them to this day but they are
unsuitable for publication in your newspaper.

Paul Cornish
Leeds, West Yorkshire

Out of the office

SIR – I read with amusement Madeline Grant's offering on "management gobbledygook".

It brought to mind an early meeting, post-sale of my small business to a large corporate, in which the head of marketing asked me to "re-purpose the existing marketing collateral", which, after questioning, translated into "use the current sales brochure".

Paul Timson
Biddulph, Staffordshire

SIR – I worked for Ford Motor Co some years back and in one office a large wall hanging declared: REPUDIATE POLYSYLLABIC MONSTROSITIES.

It always stayed with me throughout my business career.

David O'Brien
Bishop's Itchington, Warwickshire

SIR – Some years ago a colleague and I had a response when we heard management-speak in meetings by stating that what we had heard was an "LOB" statement. Not once was this challenged by the speakers, who were probably either too embarrassed or too proud to admit they didn't know what it meant.

For the record, it meant "Load Of B—-cks".

Graham Jones
Tytherington, Cheshire

Sworn testimony

SIR – Recent discussion of the c-word reminded
me of an incident some forty years ago. A pleasant
and perhaps rather unworldly lady returned to our
London office one lunchtime and described a minor
traffic accident she'd witnessed. She told us that the
taxi driver was shouting at the other motorist: "You
can't, you can't". I suspect she misheard.

John Graham-Leigh
Westbury, Wiltshire

SIR – The word used by Donald Trump, on camera,
is in frequent use on buses, in pubs and anywhere less
mature people gather. It's quite tiring.

However, maybe now people will just say "Oh
Trump off".

How much nicer that would be and the word can
revert to being rare and shocking.

Michael West
Poole, Dorset

SIR – Although I have not used the word from the
pulpit yet, I must defend our use of the word *fecking*
and its derivatives. For example, once a member of
the congregation after divine worship asked me how
my chickens were. My response was: "The fecking fox
killed them all last night." This evoked expressions of
sympathy from those who heard my reply. *Fecking* is an
expression used by, and utterly acceptable to, the most
stern matrons of the Church of Ireland.

The word is NOT to be confused with a similar-sounding word used both here and in all English-speaking nations – and with variations in German – which substitutes *u* in our word for the *e* in *fecking*. For example, a daughter of a friend who found herself working in London was once asked to do some task which would interrupt her present task. She replied: "Would ye ever feck off, I'm busy." For this she was hauled to the managing director and had to explain – very gently given the clash of cultural understandings – that this phrase simply means "give me a minute or two and I will be with you".

So, sir, let me assure you that respectable matrons and clergy freely use the word *fecking* here without the shame you assign to the word and phrase. We, sir, are not feckless. We fecking deny that. If the fecking fox fecked my fecking chickens the fecking fox had better fecking watch out.

Rev Kenyon Homfray
Fethard, Co Tipperary, Ireland

Graffiti rules OK

SIR – Many years ago I had a boss who wasn't really up to his job, resulting in quite a few comments being written on lavatory walls.

For some reason he had seen the graffiti and called us all together with the ensuing statement.

"It's come to my attention that there's lots of allegations about me written on the toilet walls and if I catch these alligators there's going to be trouble!"

Needless to say his reputation was suitably enhanced.

Anthony Bolton
Church Stretton, Shropshire

SIR – My favourite piece of graffiti read: "Preserve Wildlife – Pickle a Squirrel Today".

Ann Runacres
Ullenhall, Warwickshire

SIR – During the 1980s I was a student at the University of Southampton. I clearly remember the handwritten sign carefully attached to the toilet paper dispenser in the loos. It read: "Arts degrees – please take one".

Kate Pycock
Ipswich, Suffolk

SIR – As a young commuter to London in the early 1960s, I remember a sign at Burnham on Crouch station in the gents' toilet which stated: "VD can be cured!"

Some wag had added: "So can kippers!"

Tony Ellison
Westcliff-on-Sea, Essex

DEAR
DAILY TELEGRAPH

Every picture tells a story

SIR – Who exactly did you expect to be interested
in the article "How to spider-proof your home"?
I presume that it was intended for arachnophobes,
otherwise it would have been titled "How to introduce
more spiders into your home."

So why pepper the article with life-size photos of
the very creature which some of us find terrifying?
I, for one, squeaked as soon as I saw that page, and
could hardly touch the paper to turn to the next.

For future reference, if you decide to publish any
similar articles and feel an illustration is required,
please use a cartoon version, preferably with a big
smiley face on it and wearing a hat.

Sarah Woodley
Biddenden, Kent

SIR – Page three of today's *Daily Telegraph* is largely taken
up with a picture of four young women modelling
"stylish" clothes. If the object of the display is to
entice potential buyers, why on earth were the models'
faces so grim and sulky? Did they feel uneasy, bored,
fed up? Or were they perhaps uncomfortable in the
garments they were required to exhibit?

Frankly, having glanced at their lowering
expressions, I hastily turned my eye to the intriguing
plight of woolly mammoths at the bottom of the page.

Suzette Hill
Ledbury, Herefordshire

SIR – Please will you stop printing pictures of kissing politicians? It's putting me off my breakfast.

John Stringer
Harbury, Warwickshire

SIR – Is there any chance there might be an issue of *The Daily Telegraph* in the near future that does not feature a photograph of Rachel Reeves?

Ray Winstanley
Sheffield, South Yorkshire

SIR – Two days without a picture of Harry and Meghan.
   I'm beginning to forget what they look like.

John Oughton
Leeds, West Yorkshire

Weighing up the options

SIR – You report that the world's biggest pumpkin "could end up weighing as much as a rhino". If the rhino is a new standard of weight, does it replace the elephant? And if so, what is the elephant/rhino ratio?
   An answer in bags of sugar would be helpful.

John Spanner
Redhill, Surrey

Between the headlines

SIR – I was startled to read the headline "Pensioners could serve their time in Estonia" in *The Daily Telegraph*. Only on a second reading (and after failing to find my passport) did I realise the headline referred to "Prisoners". Still, nothing would surprise me now.

P. Sweatman
East Linton, East Lothian

SIR – I was much amused by your positioning of letters: below your array of extraction methods for avocado stones was "Excessive demands placed on grandparents".

Alistair Bishop
Northwood, Middlesex

SIR – Your article "Starmer in smoky bacon surrender to EU", chronicling the heavy hand of the EU on Britons' favourite snack flavourings, was written by one James Crisp. Is *The Daily Telegraph* scrupulously neutral in this hot topic? No smoke without fire, bacon or not.

Mart Ralph
Salisbury, Wiltshire

Praise the Lords

SIR – Others were no doubt as delighted as me to read of the outcome of the recent Lords v Commons annual bridge match, reported in Friday's edition. We were told that the House of Lords triumphed for the 28th time. Perhaps even more exciting was the final paragraph of the report which told us that:

"The Anthony Berry award for the best hand went to Lords Mendoza and Howard, who were the only pair to bid and make a small slam in diamonds, on the fifth board of the match."

I readily confess that I have absolutely no idea what that means but I take some small pleasure in the fact that I live in a country where a small slam in diamonds by their lordships is covered in the national press.

Tim Reid
Mayfield, East Sussex

Puzzles and conundrums

SIR – The answer to 28 down in the *Sunday Telegraph* Quick Crossword could quite easily have been more apt. The clue was "fool" (5). I had the first letter T and the last P. I thought it was *Trump*, but it was *twerp*. Same difference in my book.

Janet Milliken
Folkestone, Kent

The genuine article

SIR – In these days of political ineptitude and leadership elections, I would like to put forward the following for immediate appointment to run the country: Matt, Michael Deacon and Celia Walden. I am sure that between them they would bring a great deal of common sense (which in reality is not at all common), and I feel confident that we would also thoroughly enjoy ourselves at the same time.

Anthony Bagshawe
Hawes, North Yorkshire

SIR – Surely William Sitwell must be in the running for the next Archbishop of Canterbury?

Whatever shortcomings may emerge in his selection, we could at least expect advice for excellent meals after endless meetings, as opposed to decaffeinated coffee with oat milk and Digestives.

Jenny Cooke
Cambridge

No more funny business

SIR – In these dark days when almost every headline seems to augur the oncoming apocalypse, you then kill off Alex. Have you no pity – you have tipped us over the edge. It now really does feel like the Biblical End Times. I'm off to start digging a shelter and taking my Alex annuals with me.

David Cain
Tonbridge, Kent

SIR – The sad news of Alex Masterley's quiet retrenchment from the *Telegraph* marks the end of another chapter in his storied career. Given the current market maelstrom, his gardening leave appears wonderfully well-timed. I look forward to his inevitable return to the City – a banker of his skill and mastery will surely receive a flood of offers to help clients navigate the new Trumpian era. Until then, what am I to read at breakfast?

James Johnstone
London SW3

Good on paper

SIR – Whether by accident or design, the litter tray of our two chickens, Bubble and Squeak, is exactly the size of an open broadsheet newspaper. Each day, it is replaced with the previous day's *Daily Telegraph*, spread showing the cartoon, comment, editorial and readers' letters. This provides them with news, analysis, humour and the intriguing possibility of seeing their names in print.

Tom Roberts
Wing, Rutland

SIR – I read *The Daily Telegraph* online. I did not realise that this would cause a problem. I do not have a newspaper to use for cleaning the windows.

Judith Book
Crowthorne, Berkshire

Read all about them

SIR – My New Year's resolution is to get a letter published in *The Daily Telegraph*. I may not reach the success rate of my step-nephew, who got to double figures for 2024, but I am loving learning more about him through the Letters page.

Dr Suzanne Howarth
Nailstone, Leicestershire

SIR – Yesterday I joined a queue in our local well-known pharmacy to collect a prescription. Ahead of me was an elderly lady. On her hearing my name she turned to me and asked if I'd stopped writing letters to *The Daily Telegraph*. I assured her I had not but you had seen fit not to publish any.

Please would you be so kind and publish this letter, at least to assure her that I am still alive.

John Tilsiter
Radlett, Hertfordshire

SIR – I've never been to Storrington (pop. 6,000), but for a small town it produces several high-quality contributors to your Letters page. Perhaps I ought to visit, as it must have a high number of intelligent and literate citizens.

Alexander McAllister
Bournemouth, Dorset

SIR – I note that today's Letters page includes three Moores – a letter from nurse Mary Moore and a letter from Margaret Moore which refers to Mary Moore, i.e. me. Let's have more of this!

Mary Moore
Croydon, Surrey

SIR – I've been waiting patiently since the start of the year to see which David Miller would have a letter published first.

Congratulations to the one from Chigwell; where are you Tunbridge Wells?

Joanna Bunkham
Newton, Glamorgan

SIR – Your books of unpublished letters should be available on the NHS as a treatment for depression.

Unfortunately, not enough of them are by me.

Andrew H. N. Gray
Edinburgh

It's that time of year again

SIR – When is Black Friday? It seems to have been here for a month.

Pauline Hay
Epsom, Surrey

SIR – I bought my first poinsettia yesterday (November 4). However, to put it in pride of place, I had to find a new home for one I bought last year.

Is this a record?

Margaret Scattergood
Solihull, West Midlands

SIR – What is the correct sartorial wear for Yuletide?
We were at Chester station just before Christmas
and counted two Christmas trees, a penguin and a
Christmas pudding alighting from trains.

> **Jo-Ann Rogers**
> Stoke-on-Trent, Staffordshire

SIR – I recently bought my wife an advent calendar
containing her favourite chocolates. When I looked
today I was amazed to see it was December 24 already.
I must have overslept.

> **Richard Acland**
> Beachley, Gloucestershire

SIR – My wife has for some years followed what I call
the Morticia Addams School of Christmas decoration,
by bringing in a couple of dead branches from the
garden, placing them in a large vase and draping some
tinsel over them.

> **Bruce Carlin**
> Dewsbury, West Yorkshire

SIR – With the Princess of Wales revealing that she
received a chainsaw as a Christmas present, I am
reminded of the most appreciated present I ever gave
my wife – her own set of drain rods. It was capped,
a year later, with a full set of attachments.

> **Tony Hughes**
> West Marden, West Sussex

SIR – My memory regularly fails me at Christmas, particularly when I forget where I have hidden all the presents. One year having switched on the hostess trolley on Christmas Day I realised there was a strong smell permeating from it. On inspection several gifts were found to be stuck to the heated shelves. For some of us there is no hope.

Kirsty Blunt
Sedgeford, Norfolk

SIR – So that's it over for another year.

For now, the commercial and journalistic cliches and the religious platitudes will be carefully packed away for further use; the inflatable Santas and reindeers will be removed from rooftops; the miles of flashing, multi-coloured lights will be taken down from house fronts and gardens, and (with luck) turkey, Brussels sprouts and pigs-in-blankets will no longer appear on menus.

I believe that Christmas, like the Olympic Games, should only be held every four years.

Roy Bailey
Great Shefford, Berkshire